# LETTERS FROM THE BLACK SEA

DURING

THE CRIMEAN WAR, 1854—1855.

ADMIRAL
SIR LEOPOLD GEORGE HEATH, K.C.B.
1873.

# Letters from the Black Sea

DURING

THE CRIMEAN WAR, 1854—1855.

BY

ADMIRAL
SIR LEOPOLD GEORGE HEATH,
K.C.B.

*WITH ILLUSTRATIONS.*

**The Naval & Military Press Ltd**

*Published jointly by*

**The Naval & Military Press Ltd**

*In reprinting in facsimile from the original, any imperfections are inevitably reproduced and the quality may fall short of modern type and cartographic standards.*

DEDICATED

IN MY EIGHTIETH YEAR

TO

THE FEW SURVIVORS

OF MY MANY FRIENDS IN

THE BLACK SEA FLEET,

1854—1855.

# INTRODUCTION.

These letters have lain on a shelf untouched and almost unthought of for many years, but, as is the habit of old men, I took them down recently to refresh my memory of the events in which I had taken part during the most stirring times of my earlier life. They interested me much, and I publish them thinking that perhaps they may also interest others.

The earlier letters—that is, those previous to February, 1855—describe events occurring whilst I was in command of the "Niger," or of the "Sanspareil," and carrying out the ordinary duties of the service; but those of a later date were written whilst I was holding the position of Harbour Master at Balaklava or of Principal Agent of Transports.

It will be seen that the series begins with the declaration of war and ends with the fall of Sebastopol. Some few letters have been lost, but none of much consequence, except, perhaps, that which described the battle of Tchernaya, in which victory over the attacking Russians—said to have been sixty thousand strong—was won by the Sardinians, aided partially by ourselves and the French, and, I think, by a few Turks.

Many "Letters from the Crimea" and histories of the campaign have been brought before the public, but I think they have all been written by Officers of the Sister Service and that these are the first from a Sailor's pen. I have included amongst the Letters a semi-official report upon the loss of the "Prince," and also two documents and two photographs showing the real condition of Balaklava Harbour. On both these points the English newspapers used very strong language, but the "Correspondents" of those days were not the steady, history-recording gentlemen who now accompany our armies; they apparently considered that to interest and excite the readers of their newspapers was their only mission.

In the Appendix are two or three documents of interest, and it closes with the despatches from the Duke of Newcastle, after receiving reports of the first bombardment—of the battle of Balaklava—and that of Inkerman. The last-named is extraordinarily eloquent, and one cannot read its many tender and pathetic passages without a strong suspicion that although the pen was that of the Minister for War, the words were those of a more exalted person. What can be more Queen-like than "Let not any private soldier in the ranks believe that his conduct is unheeded—the Queen thanks him—his Country honours him."

It was my great good fortune to obtain the good opinion both of Admiral Dundas and of Sir Edmund Lyons, and I take this opportunity of expressing the gratitude with which I received their many acts of kindness both professional and private.

L. G. HEATH.

Anstie Grange, Holmwood.

May, 1897.

# TABLE OF CONTENTS.

## INTRODUCTION.

PAGE

### LETTER No. 1.

Declaration of War—Flag of Truce Fired at—French Generals and Turkish Pasha at Gallipoli .. .. 1

### LETTER No. 2.

"Retribution," "Descartes," and "Niger" sent to Odessa—Capture of Prizes—Reconnaisance of Bay—Appearance of the Town .. .. .. .. 6

### LETTER No. 3.

Expedition to Sulina—"Sidon" on shore and hove off by "Niger"—Anecdote of Russian Prisoner .. 11

### LETTER No. 4.

Description of Varna—Sale of Prizes—Odessa Bombarded by the Fleet—Naval Ladies at Therapia .. 16

### LETTER No. 5.

Expedition to Kaffa Bay and Circassia—"Niger" on Shore .. .. .. .. .. .. .. .. 21

### LETTER No. 6.

"Tiger," "Niger," and "Vesuvius" sent to Odessa—"Tiger" on Shore and Burnt—Captain Giffard Wounded and Died—"Niger" to Malta for Repairs 25

## CONTENTS.

PAGE

### LETTER No. 7.
"Niger" Returns from Malta—Blockades Danube—St. Sophia—Fidonisi Lighthouse—Mosquitoes—Telegraph Posts—Caught Napping—Cholera in the Fleet—Crimean Expedition decided on—Russian Fishermen .. .. .. .. .. .. .. 33

### LETTER No. 8.
Commander Tatham promoted—Loss in Fleet from Cholera .. .. .. .. .. .. .. 42

### LETTER No. 9.
Neutrals carrying Enemy's Goods—Bullock Hunt—French and Turkish portion of the Expedition Sighted—"Niger" joins the Fleet .. .. .. 44

### LETTER No. 9—*Continued.*
Advice given to Admiral Hamelin—Disposition of the Fleet of Transports .. .. .. .. .. 49

### LETTER No. 10.
Disembarkation at Old Fort—Skirmish at Bulganak—Battle of Alma .. .. .. .. .. .. 53

### LETTER No. 11.
Number of Killed and Wounded—Wounded carried down by Sailors—Flank March to Balaklava—Take possession of Balaklava—Land Guns and Stores—St. Arnaud Ill—Canrobert takes Command.. .. 63

### LETTER No. 12.
French Attempt at Walking Off with our Captured Guns—Naval Brigade Landed—French Transports leave Balaklava and take Possession of Harbours at Kamiesh .. .. .. .. .. .. .. 67

### LETTER No. 13.
Visit the Lines at Sebastopol—Increase of Fortifications—Lancaster Guns—Fortification of Balaklava—"Un Grand Malheur".. .. .. .. .. 72

## CONTENTS.

### LETTER No. 14.

Another Visit to the Lines and to a New Battery—Chances of Escape from a Bursting Shell—Male Inhabitants of Balaklava Ordered to Quit—Road to the Front .. .. .. .. .. .. 76

### LETTER No. 15.

Sanitary State of Army — Arrangements for Naval Attack—Naval Attack .. .. .. .. .. 81

### LETTER No. 16.

Naval Losses — Appearance of Fort Constantine—Russian Sortie—Contrast .. .. .. .. 86

### LETTER No. 17.

Numerical Weakness of Our Forces—Attack on Turkish Redoubts—Battle of Balaklava—Proposal to Abandon Balaklava—Wiser Counsels Prevail—Balaklava Strengthened—Am Landed in Charge of a Battery with "Niger's" Crew under Sir Colin Campbell—Night Alarms .. .. .. .. .. .. 91

### LETTER No. 18.

A Critical Week—Battle of Inkerman—Visit to the Battle Field—Description of the Battle — Heavy Sortie Against the French—Superior Numbers of the Enemy—Arrival of the Transport "Prince" with Warm Clothing and Two Thousand Men—Called in to Balaklava to help Captain Dacres .. 98

### LETTER No. 19.

Appointed Acting Captain of "Sanspareil"—Speculations as to Keeping the Appointment—Gale of Wind—Loss of Ships, including the Transport "Prince" .. .. .. .. .. .. .. 106

## CONTENTS.

### LETTER No. 20.

Gallant Capture of Russian Outwork by Captain Tryon of the Rifles—Full Description of the Storm—"Avon" Steamer—H.M.S. "Retribution" with Duke of Cambridge on Board—Arrival of Hutting and of Reinforcements .. .. .. .. .. 108

### LETTER No. 21.

Forty Additional Naval Guns Landed—Appointed Harbour Master—Officers and Crew of "Sanspareil"—My Comfortable Cabin—State of the Roads .. .. .. .. .. .. .. 113

### LETTER No. 22.

My Daily Work—Sickness Increasing in Front—Difficulties of Transport—Half Rations .. .. .. 117

### LETTER No. 23.

Promoted to Post Captain—Cholera Bad—Deaths from Cholera—Coffee Roasting—Turks Sent to Eupatoria .. .. .. .. .. .. .. .. 120

### LETTER No. 24.

Complete Breakdown of Land Transport—Cavalry used for Carrying up Provisions—Success of Coffee-roasting—Inkerman Despatch .. .. 123

### LETTER No. 25.

Visit to the Camp—Progress of Works—Firewood—Cavalry Method of Carrying Grain—Distribution of Work in the Harbour.. .. .. .. .. 126

### LETTER No. 26.

More Rain, but More Mules—Sorties—French Help—Guns going to the Front—Admiral Dundas gives up the Command—Whigs Unromantic—Speculations as to my Future Position.. .. .. .. 130

## CONTENTS. xv.

PAGE

### LETTER No. 27.
Railroad Engineer—Council of War—Description of Canrobert—Arrival of Crimean Army Royal Yacht Club Ships .. .. .. .. .. .. .. 134

### LETTER No. 28.
Cold Weather—Officers *asphyxiés* by Charcoal—Provisions Carried up on Men's Backs—Railroad—State of Balaklava Harbour .. .. .. .. 137

### LETTER No. 29.
Scandalous Paragraph in *The Times* on the State of the Harbour—Loss of the "Prince"—Build Stable for Mules—Huts—Naval Brigade Reduced .. 140

### LETTER No. 30.
Mules—Sledges—Cold Weather .. .. .. .. 148

### LETTER No. 31.
Mules—Stabling and Attendance—Bad Roads .. .. 150

### LETTER No. 32.
Leave Balaklava—Effect of Change of Air on Health—Arrival of Railway Staff—Visit to the French Lines—French Mining—Catching Russians—Feeling of the French Soldiers—Admiral Boxer's Arrival—His Ideas—Appointed Principal Agent of Transports—Sir Edmund Lyons's Letters .. .. 152

### LETTER No. 33.
General Review of the Campaign—"Une audace"—The Alma—Criticisms on Delay in Following Up—The Flank March—Badness of Reasons for not Immediately Storming the South Side—Naval Bombardment—Sidney Herbert—Mr. Filder—Want of Roads—Want of Mules .. .. .. 161

### LETTER No. 34.
Coffee-roasting Machines—Reventing Guns in Front—Numbers of the British Army .. .. .. .. 168

## CONTENTS.

### LETTER No. 35.
Stafford's Speeches in the House of Commons—Their Inaccuracy—Case of the "Candia" .. .. .. 172

### LETTER No. 36.
Policy to be Adopted by my Brother in the matter of Newspaper Attacks—Balaklava Harbour—Information about it Drawn up for my Successor—Opinion of Merchant Captains .. .. .. .. .. 174

### LETTER No. 37.
Improved Condition of Affairs—Macadamized Roads—Railway Progress—General Vinois—Land Transport Corps—Civility of Soldiers—Navvies—Preparing Floating Hospitals .. .. .. .. 183

### LETTER No. 38.
Choice of a Secretary—Admiral Boxer's Zeal—Turkish Troops brought back from Eupatoria—Opening of Fire from our Batteries .. .. .. .. .. 187

### LETTER No. 39.
"Our Own Correspondents"—Sir John McNeil—*Gobemouche* Story—The Transport "Candia"—Description of Evidence given before the Sebastopol Committee .. .. .. .. .. .. .. 191

### LETTER No. 40.
Telegraph with England Established—The Master of the "Andes," and of the "Himalaya" .. .. 195

### LETTER No. 41.
Embarkation of First Expedition to Kertch—Return of Expedition—Arrival of 18th Lancers from India—Abundance of Provisions and Stores—Louis Napoleon .. .. .. .. .. .. .. 197

### LETTER No. 42.
Sebastopol Blue Book .. .. .. .. .. .. 202

## CONTENTS.

PAGE

### LETTER No. 43.

Pellissier supersedes Canrobert—Fresh Expedition to Kertch—Advance of French and Turks into the Plain of Balaklava—Description of the flowers—Bakery Established—Mr. Soyer .. .. .. 203

### LETTER No. 44.

Assault of Redan, June 18th—Reasons of Failure—Railroad People—The Clever French in the Baidar Valley .. .. .. .. .. .. 208

### LETTER No. 45.

Attack and Capture of Malakoff by the French—Our Own Repulse at the Redan—Retreat of the Russians to the North side during the Night—Visit to the Town—Description of the Redan .. 212

### LETTER No. 46.

Another Visit to the Town—Todleben's Energy—The French Assault of the Malakoff—Pellissier's Opinion that Our Attack on the Redan was most Valuable to him as a Diversion—Description of the Docks—Wind Up—Return Home—Commission "Seahorse"—Naval Review—Return for Troops .. .. .. .. .. .. .. 218

### APPENDIX.

*Facsimile* of Lord Raglan's Handwriting—*Facsimile* of Admiral Dundas's Handwriting—*Facsimile* of Sir Edmund Lyons's Handwriting—Duke of Newcastle's Despatches on the First Bombardment; the Battle of Balaklava; and the Battle of Inkerman .. .. .. .. .. .. .. .. 223

# LIST OF ILLUSTRATIONS.

| | | |
|---|---|---|
| ADMIRAL SIR LEOPOLD G. HEATH | | FRONTISPIECE |
| | | PAGE |
| DECLARATION OF WAR | | 2 |
| ODESSA BAY | | 17 |
| LOSS OF THE "TIGER" | facing | 28 |
| ORDER OF ANCHORING OF THE FLEET | do. | 52 |
| DOUBLE BOAT | | 54 |
| LANDING OF THE EXPEDITION | facing | 54 |
| BATTLE OF ALMA | do. | 58 |
| NAVAL BOMBARDMENT | do. | 84 |
| BATTLE OF BALAKLAVA | | 93 |
| BATTLE OF INKERMAN | | 101 |
| BALAKLAVA HARBOUR (Entrance) | } facing | 142 |
| Do.  Do. (Inside view) | | |
| ("Higgledy Piggledy, Rough and Tumble") | | |
| "ZIGZAGS" | | 153 |
| STRENGTH OF THE BRITISH ARMY JAN. 26/55 | facing | 170 |
| INTERIOR OF THE REDAN | do. | 216 |
| SEBASTOPOL DOCKS | | 221 |
| FACSIMILE OF LORD RAGLAN'S HANDWRITING | | APPENDIX |
| Do.  OF ADMIRAL DUNDAS'S HANDWRITING | | Do. |
| Do.  OF SIR EDMUND LYONS'S HANDWRITING | | Do. |

# LETTERS FROM THE BLACK SEA
DURING
# THE CRIMEAN WAR—1854-55.

*LETTER No. 1.*

H.M.S. "NIGER,"
BALJIK, April 10th, 1854.

It is a bold thing to begin journal letters on such large paper but as I should like them all kept so that I may, if I return safe and sound, bind them up as a record of the Black Sea Campaign, it will be as well that they should be similar in form to Vol. I. of the "Adventures of Commander Heath." I am the most lucky fellow possible hitherto, for whilst others have been shivering, with ice on the decks, at Baljik, I have been comfortably idling at Therapia, with my ship next door to my wife; and here I am, having brought with me the declaration of war.

About a week ago a steamer passed at night through the Bosphorus, which for various reasons was generally supposed to be the "Banshee," with the said declaration of war, and in consequence one senior officer after another left to join the Admiral until I alone remained. The "Highflyer" was the last to leave the Golden Horn, at 1 p.m., on the 8th; and at 2 p.m. the real "Banshee," with the real declaration, arrived. Her Commander had to go to the Embassy first, and make a beginning with his coaling, and it was nearly six in the evening before he, with his despatches, reached me at Therapia. Mary and I had been sketching up a neighbouring valley, and were walking leisurely back (not having heard the gun that had been fired on the arrival of the despatches) when we met a midshipman running to give me the information. We got away before eight o'clock, and reached the Admiral at half-past three on the 9th.

I meant to create great excitement by coming in with the whole signal flying at once, one word at each masthead, but the telegraphic announcement had been fully believed, and the effect was not therefore so great as it would otherwise have been. When

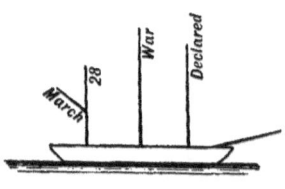

the Admiral had read his despatches he too made the signal "War is declared." The "Albion's" crew manned the rigging and cheered, followed quickly by the other ships. I have made myself hoarse with my loyalty; I gave three cheers for

## FLAG OF TRUCE FIRED AT.

the Queen, three for Old England, three for the French, three for the "Niger," and one more for Old England.

The "Furious" returned yesterday from Odessa, having been sent there to bring away the Consul. She was off the port at half-past five in the morning showing a flag of truce, and sent a boat, also with a flag of truce, to deliver the Consul's letter. The boat was told it was too early and that at six o'clock the harbour master would come out; it therefore pulled back to the ship, which was lying-to, one and a-half or two miles off. The boat was about a mile from the shore, when six successive shots from cannon were fired at her, the last being a shell; the direction of the shot was good, but they had not enough elevation, and neither the boat nor the "Furious" was touched. Captain Loring having recovered his boat, went off as hard as he could after a Russian man-of-war ten miles down to leeward, but she escaped up the Dnieper, and the "Furious" returned here —it is a pity she did not wait out of gunshot to see if the harbour master would have come out. I have this account from Captain Loring himself, and so it would seem that Russian civilisation is that of a period beyond the days of the Trojan War, for I believe heralds were even then considered sacred.

The "Fury" (you must distinguish between her and the "Furious") went off early this morning to begin work on our side by picking up anything she may find outside Sebastopol. The French steamer "Ajaccio," bringing their despatches, has not yet arrived; it is supposed her machinery has broken down, and our allies will not move without their official instructions. If the "Ajaccio" appears this afternoon we shall, I believe, all sail in the evening, but the programme of the campaign is kept secret.

Summer seems to have set in, it is almost oppressively hot to-day. We know nothing authentic about the position of the Russians, but two of our line of battle ships which have been detached at Varna are coming in, and may perhaps know something more. As to our own military operations, the works across the Isthmus at Gallipoli have already been begun.

When the French arrived their first proceedings astonished the Turks *in general*, as they named the streets and numbered the houses. The next astonished the Pasha *in particular*. Wood for the soldiers' fires was not forthcoming, and the Pasha said the wind blew too hard for the boats to cross with it from the Asiatic coast. General Canrobert answered, "If none comes in six hours I shall take your houses." And it came, but each chief has reported the conduct of the other to head quarters at Constantinople.

Our engineers are anxious to begin another Torres Vedras between Kara Bouroun on the Black

Sea and Chekinyet on the Sea of Marmora; the line is twelve miles long. General Tylden, of the Engineers has had a fall from his horse, but is recovering.

## LETTER No. 2.

H.M.S. "NIGER,"
  Finished off Fidonisi Island,
    April 18th, 1854.

I should have supposed the use of "Banshees" and "Caradocs" was to give us an advantage over our enemies by having earlier information, and that on the "Niger's" arrival strong steam squadrons would immediately have left the combined fleet, one of which might have made the southern point of the Crimea, and sweeping round by Kaffa Bay and the Circassian coast have picked up a few stray men-of-war, while the others making for the same point might have gone westward towards Odessa, and would certainly have caught a few stray merchant ships. With the exception, however, of the "Fury" being detached to Sebastopol on the morning of the 9th, no move was made until the afternoon of the 11th, when "Retribution," "Descartes," and "Niger" were started off for Odessa, where we arrived in the forenoon of the 13th. We took possession of a merchant brig lying outside, but left Russian colours flying as a decoy.

"Descartes" and "Niger" then went round the bay at a distance of something more than a mile to reconnoitre the newly-made batteries. Thousands of people were up on the cliff looking at us, and being all dressed in black or blue we at first thought they must be troops; but they were too mobbish for that.

The town seems handsomely built of stone, and is well supplied with brightly-painted domes and cupolas; the Cathedral has a tall spire. The position of the town is something like that of Brighton, but the plain on which it is built slopes rather more away from the sea. There is the same sort of cliff but a wider beach, on which are built storehouses, quarantine establishments, etc., etc., and all the new batteries are along it and on the piers, which are built out and form artificial harbours, containing some 200 sail of vessels, thirty or forty of them being English.

A brig lying about fifteen hundred yards from the beach unwisely showed Russian colours as we passed, and just as our reconnaisance was completed she began to think she had done a foolish thing and therefore slipped her chain and made sail towards the shore; the "Niger" was after her directly, and hooking her on *en passant* towed her out triumphantly, passing within twelve hundred yards of the batteries, which to our surprise did not fire. The moment the "Descartes" saw what we were up to she gallantly stood in, ready to support us had we been fired at. Modesty ought to compel me not to say that the "Retribution" made the signal "Very well done."

Meanwhile a boat had gone out to the "Retribution" to know what we had come for; Captain Drummond would give no direct answer, but asked if there was any explanation relative to the "Furious" having been fired at when her flag of truce was up; and we suppose that the forbearance shown in not firing at us arose from the Governor's knowledge that he was in a scrape for having on that occasion been too hasty with his guns. Having thus got two prizes, which were both empty, I went after a vessel coming down the Dnieper, which turned out to have about thirty tons of linseed on board.

It was arranged that the next morning the "Retribution" should remain to receive any communication that might arrive, and that we should go on towards the Dnieper, whilst 'Descartes" went towards the Dniester. Having got as far as I had been told to go, I saw ahead a Russian transport in tow of a tug, and went on in hopes of bringing in the first pendant; but she was inside the river, where I could not with any safety follow without a pilot, so I contented myself with having verified the chart as far as the very mouth of the river and with capturing six more vessels, two of them being laden with coals, and then returned to the "Retribution," which had herself taken two small craft. I showed Russian colours when chasing the transport, and was in hopes when I lowered them half-mast she would fancy me on shore and send the tug to assist me, but as she made some signal, which of course I could not answer, she naturally smelt a rat. And, indeed, as there are telegraphs all along the coast our arrival had of course been reported. A fort called Kinbourn amused itself with firing at me, but as I was three and a-half miles from it they might as well have saved their powder.

The 15th was employed in transhipping our linseed and two cargoes of oatmeal to the best of our empty brigs, and in putting the coal into the steamers. I took a fruitless cruise to Tendra, and the Frenchman picked up a fine brig laden with salt. Our orders obliged us to return to the rendezvous off the Island of Fidonisi. Whilst *en route* I descried a large schooner, which I chased on shore and sent the boats in to destroy, she was a fine, well-found vessel, laden with salt. We helped ourselves to all sorts of little useful articles, and then set her on fire. I walked off with her bell and intend setting it up at Moorhurst, also a little deal whatnot, the very image of the one Julia has there, and I intend it to take its place in the same corner.

It seems barbarous work capturing all these little vessels, but it is the only way of stopping the trade, which is what we want to do. I don't suppose another vessel will show outside their harbours for some time, and the inhabitants of the coast from the Dnieper to the Dniester will bear no good-will to their Emperor for the sufferings they will in consequence be subjected to.

April 17th.—The "Sidon" has arrived and carries off the "Retribution" and "Descartes" to attack the batteries at the Sulina mouth of the Danube. I am to remain in case the Admiral should arrive at the rendezvous, however as they are specially ordered not to land or in any way to expose their ships to danger, I don't much regret being left. The battery mounts only six guns, but there are some gunboats also. Even supposing they succeed to the utmost extent they will, in my opinion, have done nothing useful, for as soon as they are gone the Russians may begin and build doubly strong forts, and it seems to me a mere waste of coal, powder, and shot.

April 18th.—The steamers left last night but returned this morning, the weather being too bad to make the attempt, smooth water being a necessary element for successful target practice at two thousand yards distance.* The "Sidon" returns to her station and we despatch one of our full prizes to Constantinople, and I suppose await the arrival of the fleet. I am quite full of coal, thanks to the prizes. The "Fury" took a man-of-war schooner off Sebastopol, but was chased by a superior force and had to let go the prize; From prisoners she learnt that fourteen Russian line of battle ships were ready for us.

---

* In those days the guns were smooth-bore.

*LETTER No. 3.*

———

H.M.S. "NIGER,"

April, 1854.

April 19th.—A fine calm day. "Sidon" came in again at eight o'clock, and Captain Goldsmith made arrangements with Captain Drummond that "Descartes" and "Retribution" were to go in with him to attack the forts and gunboats at the Sulina mouth of the Danube, and that I was to remain at the rendezvous. Now as the others are all post-captains it was clear that, supposing the expedition successful and considered wise at head quarters, I should lose my promotion by remaining, and that being the only Commander present I should not interfere with anyone else's prospects by going. So I represented this to Goldsmith, and he at once acceded to my coming. I accordingly hurried off the prize brig which I was to send to Constantinople, and away we all went and arrived at Sulina at half-past two.

It had been arranged that Goldsmith should anchor first, and that we were to take positions in certain directions from him afterwards. When close in, "Retribution" boarded an Austrian and heard that the forts had been deserted two days before, and that the gunboats and troops had all gone up the river at the same time. This was signalised to the "Sidon," which ship had, however, now got into her position; but she had gone in too close and was hard and fast aground within seventeen hundred yards of the forts. A pretty mess she would have been in if the Russians had not so opportunely left the coast clear; as it was she would have been awkwardly placed had the "Niger" not been there, for neither the "Retribution" nor "Descartes" could have got near enough to give any assistance, except with boats. However, drawing less water, we were able to anchor near enough, and after three hours' anxiety had the satisfaction to heave her off.

It is clear I am in the end to be promoted for helping my friends and not for hurting my enemies. Russian transports and Russian forts come near enough to make one's mouth water, but no more; and this is the third time within six months that I have got my friends out of their difficulties.

Thursday, 20th.—Having returned to our rendezvous, I was doing some repairs to the engine whilst the others were examining Fidonisi Island, when in comes the "Sidon" again, but accompanied this time by the "Furious," which had been sent from the squadron. Her orders were to send "Retribution" and "Descartes" to Odessa, whither the Admirals had gone, and poor "Niger" was to join "Sidon" and "Firebrand" in their blockade of the coast between Danube and Varna. "One never knows whether one travels too fast or too slowly," is an old saying. Had I remained at the rendezvous instead of going to the Sulina forts I should have seen the Admiral as he passed, and should doubtless have been taken on with him to Odessa, as I had attained some local knowledge of its environs. They say there is nothing whatever to be done at my new station, whereas up there there was the Dnieper to be followed up, the Odessa batteries to be hammered down (if they did not first come to terms), and the Dniester lake to be scoured with boats— besides a little bullock hunt which might, I think, have been made with safety and success, and perhaps a great heap of money in the shape of a ransom from the town of Odessa to save it from bombardment! On the other hand, the "Sidon" might now have been a wreck, and I should have been without what little credit I may have got for getting her off.

April 21st.—Off the Sulina again, on my way to Kustendji; boarded a number of vessels—nothing new. They assure me three hundred thousand Russians have gone into Bulgaria but that they will not advance until May, as there is as yet no grass for the horses. They say they are fortifying the St. George mouth of the river; I cannot understand their reason for doing so, unless they are expecting some boat expedition of ours up there, or that we should attempt to land our army in that neighbourhood. I don't know what our troops are about, but our navy certainly seems to me to be wasting its time. My plan would be to have taken the whole fleet to Sebastopol first, then to leave a large portion of it to blockade the Russians effectively, and from that point to start off steam squadrons right and left. I believe had we followed this plan we should by now have entirely stopped Russian commerce in the Black Sea and have destroyed almost every boat belonging to them. Our little squadron being ordered to remain only sixty hours before Odessa (for fear of a superior Russian force coming from Sebastopol), we had just begun to see our way when we had to leave the place, and not a vessel of ours has yet been sent east of Sebastopol.

However, you will think, and perhaps rightly, —"It is all very well for you to talk, who have not the responsibility of managing the fleet on your shoulders." Still my bare narrative of facts without digressions and opinions would be stupid. We have fifty-one prisoners from our prizes, half on board "Retribution" and half on board "Descartes"; they are quite happy, and the only complaint made against them is their dirt. They are distributed amongst the sailors' messes in the former ship, and the other day the first lieutenant heard in the morning one of the sailors call out "I say, Jack, have you seen my Rooshan messmate, I can't find him nowhere and I wants to give him a wash."

April 22nd, Kustendji.—The "Firebrand" is here with nothing new; shooting at Cossacks is their daily amusement, but no personal damage has yet been done on either side.

April 26th.—At Varna, but no time to describe it. The "Terrible" has arrived with news of the destruction of the Imperial Mole at Odessa, with next to no loss to us and little or no damage to the town.

*LETTER No. 4.*

H.M.S. "NIGER,"

April, 1854.

April 27th.—Left Varna to return to Kustendji. Varna is situated at the mouth of a wide valley bounded to the north and south by ranges of high hills, but these hills being long beyond gun shot reach, the position seems to me well chosen for a good strong place. The town is entirely surrounded by a rampart and dry ditch, with redoubts at intervals armed with heavy cannon, and there are besides four strong outworks. The whole number of guns mounted is one hundred and ninety.

I had a sale by auction of the prizes, but only got about £600 for the whole six. Only two were at all sound, and there were no buyers for the other four. I had always said I should be quite contented with anything above £500, but the sanguine dispositions expected a great deal more. The sale was made by the Consul, and when it was all over he got into a great fright at what he had done, for there is no doubt in law that those vessels are not yet mine and that they should by rights have been kept until condemned and made

## THE "MOLE" BATTERIES.

lawful prizes by the proper Court. However, I believe there is no real risk as long as there is no doubt about the vessels, which there is not in this case. The only doubt is as to what amount of evidence may be required by the Vice-Admiral's Court to condemn upon. We have sent an officer with the papers to Malta, but they may require to see the vessels themselves.

We have just boarded an English vessel from Odessa; she and six others came out in the confusion of the attack. You will, of course, have all the details of the business in the newspapers long before this. It seems that the batteries on the Imperial Mole were entirely destroyed, and that sixteen Russian ships were burnt or sunk. According to our reconnaisance this is the plan of

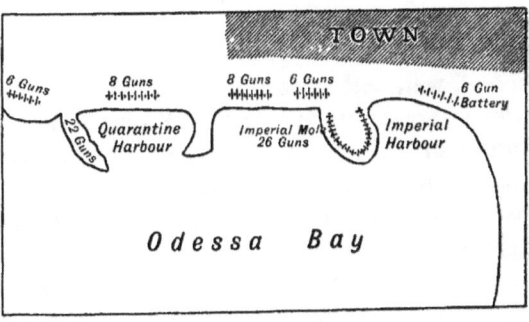

the batteries, but we could only count the embrasures, and cannot say whether there were guns in them. The smallness of our loss is surprising, and shows what advantage there is in having long heavy guns to oppose to shorter and lighter ones. The Admiral most skilfully contrived that if there were to be any Commander promoted it should be his own, for he had all of us out of the way and sent Dickson in charge of the "Rocket" boats. This vessel saw the "Fury" two hours ago; no doubt she is looking for us, and I am in great hopes of getting a new station.

April 29th.—Arrived at Kustendji, where I found orders to go on with the "Retribution" and "Firebrand" to join the squadron off Sebastopol. We only stopped an hour, and with a fair wind reached the squadron on the evening of the 30th. The Russians are still in harbour. Sir Edmund Lyons is waiting the return of the "Terrible," with Circassian interpreters, to go with a squadron —of which "Niger" forms a part—to the Circassian Coast, but according to present arrangements I go only as far as Kaffa Bay. The squadron on the way down scoured the coast and took a few prizes as they came along. A Russian man-of-war steamer came out from Sebastopol yesterday evening and had a look at us at a distance, retreating when followed I hope the Admiral will now be persuaded to blockade this place more effectively. It seems every one gives the same advice to him. I did my small best in the same direction after breakfasting with him this morning. There are but fourteen line of battle ships at the outside in Sebastopol, and we might therefore easily detach two or three liners at a time for refreshing, provisioning, etc., whilst steamers might go east and west and scour the sea and its shores until not a fishing boat remained, and the Black Sea would certainly then no longer be a Russian lake.

The Admiral seems very pleased with the exertions of the "Retribution" squadron off Odessa, and actually wanted to reward me by a trip to Constantinople. Fortunately Sir Edmund Lyons was there to object, and to point out that it would be the worst thing he could do for me, and that he should, on the contrary, give me every opportunity of earning my promotion. Admiral Dundas tells me he has again written to the Admiralty in my favour, but did not say whether with reference to getting the "Sidon" off or only in general terms. However every little helps, and I shall be disappointed if I am many months more without the third stripe.

I shall leave this letter behind, as opportunities are more frequent from the flagship than from detached ships. I have nothing more to tell you in the public or historical line, and will turn to domestic affairs. Mary is now as safe at Therapia as she could be anywhere, for Greek revolutionists and English troops are not likely to co-exist there; she will therefore remain for the present and enjoy the delights of Bosphorus spring, and of our weekly, or at all events very frequent, correspondence. They have a very snug little coterie of naval ladies there, of whom Lady Emily is the centre, and they, barring their widowhood, are not so very much to be pitied; while, as one cannot expect always to make war pay for war by taking the enemy's coals, we must sooner or later go back to replenish. I believe my share of prize-money up to this time is about £50.

Finished,

    May 1st, 1854,

        Off Sebastopol.

*LETTER No. 5.*

H.M.S. "NIGER,"

Off Sebastopol, May, 1854.

May 2nd.—Hove to with the fleet twenty miles south-west of Sebastopol, waiting for the "Terrible" to return from Constantinople with the Circassian interpreters. How odd it seems that with railroads, electric telegraphs, Consuls, and free trade, you should be obliged to send a man-of-war to dig through the ice as far as Revel to know whether seven or eight line of battle ships were or were not wintering there. Sir Edmund Lyons is much pleased with his son's performance, and well he may be, but I cannot help thinking an advertisement in *The Times* would have brought the requisite information without all that trouble. I don't think you need be much excited on the subject of the Black Sea Fleet. We seem to me rather inclined to go to sleep, and I expect the principal part of our work will be carrying the troops about from point to point. Sir E. Lyons will, I daresay, do something when he gets to the eastward, but time is everything in naval wars, as in others, and every week spent here means, I suppose, another battery added by our enemies to their defences.

Personal communication with the combatants at Odessa has not given me anything new to add to the account I gave you in my last, except that from the position taken up by our steamers there were not more than five guns at the most—*viz.*, those situated at the extremity of the Imperial Mole, which could be brought into play by the Russians. It shows how formidable even one or two guns in a well made battery may be to shipping at a long distance. If I remember rightly it was a small battery of four or five guns only which took the line of battle ship in the Schleswig-Holstein war—the tables might perhaps be turned if a great big line of battle ship were to get close alongside the battery.

May 4th.—The "Terrible" arrived, bringing a mail, but no letter for me from England, and no newspaper less than five weeks old.

May 5th.—Started with the "Agamemnon," "Sampson," "Retribution," "Highflyer," and "Firebrand" for the east. The "Charlemagne," "Mogadore," and "Vauban" were to have been waiting for us at a certain rendezvous, but we had to wait there a day for them, for they had somehow or other got adrift. We all went to Sir Edmund Lyons on the 6th and received our

respective orders—" Highflyer," " Firebrand," and
" Niger" were to sink, burn, and destroy in
Kertch Bay, whilst a simultaneous process was to
be carried on by the rest of the squadron in Kaffa
Bay.

We parted company from Sir Edmund, and
Moore's squadron arrived at its destination on the
morning of the 8th, and on rounding Cape Takti
saw two vessels beating out, one of which immediately on seeing us bore up, and of course made
us think her a Russian. My signal was made to
chase, and off I went, trusting to a new chart from
a Russian survey just sent out to us; I had also
a Turkish pilot on board, but nevertheless was
very shortly hard and fast on a ledge of rocks,
projecting considerably further from the shore
than the chart marks. We were going eight knots
and the rocks were cruelly hard, and our keel
ground along from the mainmast to the stern.
After five hours hard work, and with the cordial
assistance of Moore and Parker, with their ships
and ships' companies, we hauled off, after nearly
six hours' detention. Some ugly pieces of wood
floated up, one of which the carpenter takes to be
a piece of the stern, and the ship must be docked.
Neither ourselves or the Kaffa Bay expedition
found any prizes. Sir Edmund Lyons gave me
all possible consolation and told me how often he
had got on shore himself, and that in his opinion
no small craft Captain could be worth much who

did not get on shore occasionally; he also quoted a famous letter of Lord Nelson's on the same subject.

May 11th.—Back with the fleet and writing in a great hurry. The Admiral laughs at my misfortune, and I am to go to Odessa with "Tiger" and "Vesuvius" to look round, and then to Constantinople to be docked. We coasted along the Crimea yesterday, from St. Theodosia to Aloupka, and I am clear for killing this sick man and taking his Crimea instead of the other sick man's Candia. The country is beautiful, and there are numbers of noblemen's houses all ready for Lord Dundas, Lord Heath, etc. (I must keep off the rocks though.) Sir Edmund has gone on to Circassia, but I believe only to open up a communication with Schamyl and not to take any active steps for the present.

I have had no letter from any of you for six weeks; I suppose it is the fault of the Post Office.

*LETTER No. 6.*

H.M.S. "NIGER,"

Off Odessa,

May, 1854.

May 13th.—One does not realise what war really is until one has either suffered oneself or seen its sad effects on one's friend. "Tiger," "Niger," and "Vesuvius" left the fleet, as I told you in my last letter, to look in to Odessa and see if anything could be picked up in the way of prizes. We left about noon on the 11th, and went on full speed. Captain Giffard, being senior officer, made us some signals as to what course he should steer during the night, and told us in case of parting company to rendezvous at Odessa. About six in the evening he was five or six miles ahead of me (for the "Niger" does not seem to go the faster for having her keel roughened and knocked about by the rocks), and we were obliged to stop half an hour to put something to rights in the machinery, so that when we were ready to proceed he must have been about ten miles ahead; and besides that a regular Black Sea fog had come on, so that one could not see the ship's length. I therefore gave up all idea of keeping company, and steered my own course for Odessa, arriving there in the morning and stopping the engines until the fog should clear up. We had heard the firing of guns occasionally in the direction of the shore, but knowing there was a large garrison at Odessa we concluded it was their exercise day. The guns were not continuous enough for an engagement, and it was natural to suppose that if either of our companions was on shore the last thing they would do would be to fire guns, as their anxiety would be to avoid drawing attention to their state.

The fog cleared up at half-past eleven, and we found ourselves in the middle of Odessa Bay, not a mile from the Moles. I believe I have before mentioned finding a quantity of luggage belonging to Admiral Kornilaff on board one of the captured brigs; this luggage I had unfortunately turned over to the "Retribution," thinking she would be the first ship here, but I had written a note explaining all about it to the Governor of Odessa, and this note I put on board a Dutch brig which was close to me when the fog rose. Whilst the boat was away I discovered the "Tiger" on shore, five miles to the southward. I had to wait ten minutes for the boat, and then went on as hard as I could to her assistance. The "Vesuvius" came up from the southward just before me. We saw the poor "Tiger" within thirty yards of the beach, over which rose cliffs a hundred and twenty feet high, crowned by no end of Russian field pieces and troops, the former shelling the "Tiger." We opened our fire as soon as we had got within range, but it was clear the "Tiger" was in the enemy's hands, for she had no colours up; she made no answer to my signal "How can I assist you?" and no return to the Russian guns, nor could we see anyone on board. The Russian fire was therefore probably intended to lure us to closer quarters, or perhaps to tempt our boats in to bring off the crew. However, Powell, the Commander of the "Vesuvius," came on board and said he thought he had seen the "Tiger's" crew marching up the hill side, and so as nothing more was to be done and there was no object in merely exchanging shots with the field pieces, we steamed out of range and ceased firing. Smoke then began to rise from the "Tiger," and she was very soon in a blaze fore and aft; whether her own crew or the Russian shells had done it we don't know. In any case it was the best thing that could have happened, for with a garrison at Odessa of thirty thousand men and the ship thirty yards from the beach it would have been absurd to attempt and impossible to succeed in getting her off. I then hoisted a flag of truce and sent in a note to the Russian Commander asking for information about the crew. My boat was met half way by one from the shore, whose officer promised an answer should be sent, and explained (as well as a man speaking in Italian could to one who only understood English) that one officer (who turned out to be Captain Giffard) and one sailor were killed and three wounded, and that the rest were all prisoners, that the guns were all thrown overboard and the ship full of water. I waited for three hours, but no answer came. In the meantime the fire was doing its work, the masts fell in succession, and the whole of the upper works were in flames.

The poor "Tigers" seem to have done their best to get off, their boats were out and they had laid out a stern anchor and thrown their guns overboard; but it is difficult to account for their being all made prisoners, unless it was that they were so hard at work that they did not observe the rising of the fog in time to get away. Doubtless the first thing they saw was an overwhelming force almost over their heads; still I should have thought they would have taken to their boats and risked the chance of being shot in preference to the certainty of a prison.

The thick fog again came on at six, and I left to return to the Admiral. We had three men slightly wounded by shrapnel, but none of any consequence; several balls struck the ship's side, but only those coming through the ports could do much harm at that distance. Poor Mrs. Giffard is at Malta with her children. The first

LOSS OF "THE TIGER," May 12th, 1854.
"VESUVIUS." "NIGER." "TIGER."

lieutenant and surgeon are lately married, but one's sympathies are always more strong for those one knows than for strangers. It is altogether a most sad business, and I don't know when I have passed a more unhappy evening than I did last night. The only consolation is that although we have lost a ship the Russians have not gained one. I suppose they will in the course of time be able to dive for the engine, but it will be none the better for having been in salt water. I suppose experience will make us careful; the "Sidon" and "Niger" but narrowly escaped the "Tiger's" fate, they were neither of them so close to the shore, but both were well within range, and if guns had been brought down in any numbers they must probably have been abandoned. The fogs are wonderfully thick, but still we *ought* of course to be guided by the lead, and feel our way the more carefully.

I have been now all day at the rendezvous; I am with the "Vesuvius" in a sort of ring of clear water, with massive solid fog almost all round the horizon. Where the Admiral is I cannot guess. I am anxious to find him soon that he may send home the true account of this unhappy business before Russian exaggerations can reach England.

May 15th.—I found the Admiral this morning, thick fogs have kept the fleet immovable for the last two days. He was much affected by the news I brought him, and the French Admiral, to whom he sent me, also showed much sympathy. In the course of the afternoon the Admiral sent off two steamers to Odessa with, I believe, a letter to the Governor about the prisoners. They returned this afternoon, the 16th, and report that Captain Giffard lost his left leg, his nephew of the same name, a midshipman, was killed, and that the Captain and three or four of the men have since died of their wounds. They ran on shore at half-past five in the morning and were taken at half-past ten, but no further particulars could be gleaned; the Russians were very civil, and they suppose the prisoners will be well treated. It is a satisfaction to know the guns I heard were not the "Tiger's," although my conscience would under any circumstances be quite clear, for had I stood in towards them I should not have gone into shoaler water than six fathoms, which is more than half a mile from the shore, and as one could not see twenty yards on account of the fog I should not have seen the "Tiger."

May 17th.—I have now seen the first lieutenant's official report. They were unmolested until nine o'clock, when musketry began at them but did no damage; then came field pieces, which at first fired only at the masts and rigging, but at ten o'clock began at the ship and set her on fire in a few minutes. Most of the crew were down trying to put the fire out when the shot was fired which took off Giffard's leg and wounded the others, and it was clear that further resistance was useless. It was even then so foggy that the Russian ensign which they hoisted in token of submission could not be seen, and they had to send an officer in a boat with a white flag to state they had surrendered. Neither the official letter nor any of those from the prisoners which I have seen hint at the idea of getting away in the boats, and that part of the story is still a mystery. The soundings on this part of the coast are very regular, and the getting on shore was perfectly inexcusable, but it is known that when the "Tiger" left the fleet Giffard was suffering from a bad attack of fever, and it is said that when he went to bed he left orders to be called when they got into ten fathoms, and that when so called he said, "Call me when you get into eight fathoms," and then "Call me when in six fathoms," and before the officer who called him could get on deck again the ship was aground. So that "fever" lost the ship. But what was the navigating officer doing all this time? In the effort to get off there was a strange illustration of the truth of the proverb that "A little knowledge is a dangerous thing." An anchor was laid out astern, but instead of bringing its cable straight through the stern port to the capstan it was taken round the bows and brought back to the capstan through the hawse pipe, under the extraordinary idea that by so doing the heaving off power of the capstan would be doubled. The officer who directed this arrangement had been to the Naval College, and I suppose had gone through a course of lectures showing that pulleys could be made to multiply power, but he had misread or forgotten the principle. The fleet went on to Baljik for water and provisions, and I kept company with them and left for Constantinople and Malta on the 22nd.

Scurvy has shown itself in the fleet, and Baljik beef is so bad that it is not likely to cure it. A couple of ships at a time must be sent to the Bosphorus. Two forts, Poti and Redoubt Kale, have fallen to Sir Edmund Lyons, but as far as I can understand they made no resistance. I picked up Mary at Therapia and left with her on the 26th for Malta to repair, and am still *en route*.

*LETTER No. 7.*

H.M.S. "NIGER,"

Ended August 18th, 1854,

Off the Danube.

You know by this time that I left Malta on the 23rd July, 1854, towing the transport "Arthur the Great" full of bread, and that on nearing the Doro passage I saw the transport "Shooting Star" with a foul wind, and that knowing her to be laden with mules I dropped the bread and took the mules in tow. I arrived at Constantinople on the 30th of July, remained coaling until the 2nd of August, and then with the "Apollo" storeship in tow joined the Admiral at Baljik on the 3rd of August. Whilst at Constantinople I took Richard Crofton (who is spending a month on board on leave from Malta) to see the lions, and first and foremost of course stood St. Sophia. You know that until quite recently a firman has been a necessary preliminary to getting in, but times are changed and we put a bold face on and walked straight to the door, took off our boots, and wandered about quite unmolested. I think Captain Eden's prophecy will come to pass after all. He says that he expects in a few years people will be driving in hansom cabs to St. Sophia to hear a popular preacher. I discovered something new to buy in the bazaars this time—Turkish towels; you get them of a good size for two shillings each.

I found most of the fleet at Balchik, but a few vessels were at Varna assisting in the disembarkation of troops and stores. There is cholera amongst the troops at Varna, much worse with the French than the English; there have been a few cases amongst the men-of-war, and there again the French are the worst off. The much-talked-of expedition to the Crimea does not seem in favour with the big-wigs, principally, I believe, from want of positive information as to the Russian forces likely to be opposed to us, but partly from uncertainty as to Austria's intentions; and indeed I suppose it would be rash for sixty thousand men to land in an enemy's country if there were a hundred thousand troops ready to oppose them, and a very strong fortress into the bargain. One thing is quite clear, that if they go at all no more time must be lost.

I landed on the evening of the 5th for a walk. The watering place is the mouth of a fine stream of water which we traced up to its source, the road passing through orchards and vineyards, the nearest whereof will, I suppose, as the fruit ripens be plucked by the boat's crews of the watering parties. On returning I found the steam getting up, and that I was ordered to the blockade of the Danube, recalling the "Sidon" and "Highflyer." I reached them on the 7th, and as I had brought instructions for them to load their ships with timber which is lying on the beach at the mouth of the river, their Captains, Goldsmith and Moore, with Crofton and myself went on shore to start the working parties and to look about us. The lighthouse, which has been respected hitherto, is a capital place on which to establish a look out; it is 70 feet high and from the gallery at the top you look out on a flat reedy plain, the delta of the river, too swampy for human creatures to walk on, and as therefore enemies could only come to the attack *via* the paths or the river, your working parties are quite secure when once your spy has got his glass and flag to the top of the lighthouse. We saw no enemy and carried off unmolested as much timber as the vessels could take. I got under weigh before dark, to avoid the clouds of mosquitoes which were reported to have attacked the other two ships the previous night; for whatever honour and glory there might be in awaiting the attack of a body of Russian cavalry I am sure I should not have got promotion for boldly awaiting the attack of Russian mosquitoes, and bad rest at night is weakening and harassing both for officers and men.

August 11th.—I have been cruising under sail, sighting the three principal mouths as often as possible. On the 9th I made sure I saw a brig sail down the Kilia and anchor near the mouth. I stood out to sea as if I had not seen her and stood in again the next day in hopes of finding her outside, but the weather being clearer I saw it was the parish church with two towers, each with a number of stories representing top-sails, top-gallant sails, and royals, which I had mistaken for a brig.

August 12th.—There are signal posts at every two miles all along the coast between the Danube and Odessa; these posts we have always supposed to be for telegraphs, and as the carrying of stores from Odessa coastwise to the Danubian army, would, of course, be much facilitated by the notice which these telegraphs might communicate of the temporary absence of our blockading ships, I thought it would be a good thing to destroy a lot of them and thus break the continuity of the line. This morning being calm and suitable for landing I stood slowly in as far as five fathoms, which brought me fairly within range of one of them, and manned all the boats. Cossacks and foot soldiers were hovering about, and owing to the ridgy nature of the beach no satisfactory estimate of their numbers could be made; as therefore I think one should always in such cases make use of *all* the means at one's command and risk as little as possible, I commenced operations by sending them a small number of sixty-eight and thirty-two pounder shot from the ship guns, and left directions for a broadside to be fired just before we landed. This was done accordingly, and we landed and chopped down our post without opposition. After we had returned on board I saw a Russian officer ride along the beach and talk for a moment to every soldier he met; the result of the conference always was that the soldier's musket was fired off, and I suppose the object must have been to enable the officer to make a grand report to his superior. Thus ended our grand "Battle of the Beacon." (Do you remember the cartoon in Westminster Hall with that title?) The post, however, turned out not to be a telegraph, but only a rough spar with a tarred hay band wound round it, so that it could not send telegraphic messages, but could only make some one single signal; and as any bonfires made of rubbish, collected immediately our backs were turned, would answer the enemy's purpose just as well as the posts we might have cut down, I have given up the notion of destroying any more.

August 14th.—There was great excitement at four o'clock this morning, the officer of the watch rushing down to my cabin—"Three vessels close to us, Sir; two of them steamers." "Beat to quarters and get steam up"; and as soon as I had dressed and had one look at them I hunted out

the private signal and felt a good deal relieved
when I saw one of the vessels with the proper flag
up, for owing to too great a love for economy the
fires had been allowed to burn down too low, and
had our friends been Russians they would have
been much too close to be pleasant before the
engines could have been worked. "Experientia
docet," and I shall be less pennywise in future and
always be ready for anything just before daylight.
They turned out to be the "Sidon," "Vesuvius,"
and "Spitfire"; the first and last come for a cargo
of timber, which is to be picked up in large rafts
at the Sulina mouth — Wallachian property, I
suppose. Poor inhabitants of the Principalities,
they suffer from both sides!

The "Vesuvius" remains under my orders.
They bring bad news, the cholera which has
already committed great havoc amongst the troops
has now broken out on board the fleets. They
have all got under weigh and are cruising, which
is the best thing they could do, but the outbreak
seems to have been very sudden and very fatal.
The "Montebello" lost forty men in twenty-four
hours, one steamer, the "Furious" has lost eleven,
"Vesuvius" and "Sidon" had each lost one, and
expected the death of two or three more. We
have none attacked yet, and as soon as we have
finished our job of helping to load these two
vessels I shall get under weigh and never anchor
unless when necessary; indeed, as the Danube has

three principal mouths, which should all receive daily visits, anchoring off any one of the mouths could hardly be called blockading the river. Captain Goldsmith tells me that the Crimean expedition was decided on and the embarkation about to take place when the scourge broke out, and that it is now out of the question until next spring. How strange that it should have attacked all the fleets and armies engaged in this war both here and in the Baltic. I have not by-the-bye heard of it in Sebastopol, but Cronstadt is I see by the papers suffering from it.

August 16th.—Too much swell for getting into the river as yet, and we have been cruising in the offing. This morning I saw some Russian fishermen unwarily plying their trade a good way off shore and sent my boats after them. After a long chase they caught two boats with five men, but such men none of you ever saw; they were dressed in trousers and frocks of the most coarse description, ragged and filthy to an extraordinary degree —the Chinese fishermen dress like princes in comparison—their faces were quite covered with hair, and I am sure the Russians (barbarous as they are) have no barbers! My object in sending for these gentlemen was to endeavour to find out if there was any communication going on between Odessa and the Kilia by sea and what had become of the eighty Russian gunboats said to be in the Danube, for if the army leaves the banks of the river I suppose they will try and smuggle these vessels to Odessa. But my friends seem to have been brought up amongst fish, to have lived amongst fish, and to be but little above them in intelligence, so I could get nothing out of them in that line and had to put up with two fine sturgeon, one weighing 309 lbs. I paid them what was supposed to be a fair price, rather against their will, for they said, " If you take the fish it is all very well, but if you buy it from us we shall get beaten when we land." They enjoyed biscuit and pea soup amazingly, but whether it was a fast day or whether they had imbibed the prejudices of their Mussulmen neighbours I don't know, for they would neither touch pork or biscuit which had been on the same plate with it. We flatter ourselves they left with a good opinion of the English character, at all events of the English pea soup, and I hope and think the poor fellows will, if they keep their own counsel, escape their anticipated beating, for they could hardly have been seen from the shore.

August 18th.—Yesterday was fine enough for us to work at our timber loading. The "Spitfire" went inside the river with our boats and came out in the evening with an immense collection. Whilst inside, the mast-head look-out reported some Cossacks, and the "Spitfire's" officers went up and counted five dodging amongst the high reeds within half a mile of us. We thought this unsafe for our stragglers, and a gun was fired from the "Spitfire" in the direction they were supposed to be which by good fortune killed one of their horses, so we shall have instilled a salutary fear of our guns into the minds of these people without having killed anything but a horse. I have come to the end of my paper and the end of my news. We remain as yet free from all choleraic symptoms, and as I intend to keep at sea I think we have every chance of remaining clear. Richard Crofton is picking up strength. The thermometer has been down as low as 72 deg. and commonly averages 76 deg., and the weather is very fine. We want our letters more than anything else; I suppose the next arrival will bring us some.

*LETTER No. 8.*

---

H.M.S. "NIGER,"

Off the Danube,

August 27th, 1854.

In these cholera days I shall lose no opportunity of writing, although on looking at the place I write from you will hardly expect news. We have not a symptom of the malady on board, and it seems to have left our colleague, the "Vesuvius," for they have been a full week without fresh cases. The climate is very pleasant, thermometer varying from 65 to 75 degrees, and there is scarcely a day passes without some event to enliven the monotony of mere blockading. Yesterday we sent a boat six miles off to a fisherman's boat which, with one man in it, had drifted out to sea. The current was too strong for him to pull to the ship, and the officer of the watch fortunately had his glass on him when, having resigned himself to his fate, he left off pulling and began making those prostrations and gesticulations with which Easterns accompany their prayers. Had he not prayed, the officer of the watch would have supposed him to be fishing.

The embarkation has begun at Varna; I cannot help thinking it much too late in the season for Sebastopol, and that Odessa is its real destination, with perhaps an excursion thence to Nicolaev. However, all the world talks of the Crimea. Tatham, the only Commander in command senior to me has just got a death vacancy from the Admiral, which is a good thing for me. Cholera by the last accounts has almost died away in the fleet, but they must have lost upwards of four hundred men.

*LETTER No. 9.*

Finished off the Danube,

Expeditionary Fleets in sight,

September 8th, 1854.

My last was sent off by the "Sidon," August 19th, when I was left with the "Vesuvius" to carry out the blockade of the Danube. On the evening of the 21st we boarded a Tuscan brig from Odessa, bound to Constantinople with the ordinary cargo of linseed and wool and an extraordinary one of rope and sail canvas piled up on her decks; no doubt all Russian property, but according to the Order in Council such property, once on board a neutral ship cannot be touched. I should like to know what arguments can be brought to show the propriety of this arrangement. I can understand that it may be expedient to endeavour to win neutrals to our side by granting them this boon, but the practical effect must, it seems to me, be that unless we establish a blockade the whole world except England— enemy and all—may trade and make money and

## DEALING IN BULLOCKS.

pay custom house duties at any Russian port. The only merchants who suffer loss are the English, and we prohibit them from doing that which we allow the enemy to do.

The cholera still hangs about the "Vesuvius," and as she has been off and on this blockade for the last two months her crew have been fed a good deal on salt meat and want a change, so on the 22nd August I anchored at the St. George's mouth and landing with three boats opened a communication with some natives who promised to sell us bullocks the next day. The 23rd it was too stormy to land, but on the 24th the boats went in; the natives, however, had then changed their mind, and said they were afraid of the Russians, and we came away unsuccessful. In the evening we communicated with "Terrible," "Fury," and "Retribution," the two former on their return from a reconnaissance of Sebastopol, the latter on her way to Odessa to exchange a few more men for "Tiger's." They report the Russians working hard at the land defences of Sebastopol. They brought us some letters and the news of Tatham's promotion, vice Captain Smith of the "Simoom," dead of cholera. The cholera seems to have nearly ceased both with the fleet and army, the fleet having lost somewhere about four hundred men. Tatham's promotion leaves me the senior Commander in command on the station.

On the 26th we picked up a Russian fisherman twelve or fourteen miles off the land, without any paddles or anything to eat. Dunn came to me in the morning at daylight to report this boat in sight, and made one or two successive reports about her, all tending to show that the poor fellow was adrift and not merely fishing, and I directed a boat to be sent after him, for the last report was —" He has given up pulling, and I can just make out that he is bowing and crossing himself and kowtowing." It was not until a day or two afterwards that his real story came out; it was that he was drunk the previous evening and had launched his canoe to come off to the ships, and soon drifted out with the current, having only a bit of plank to paddle with. Out of gratitude for being rescued he showed us where there was a herd of bullocks, and on the 28th we landed with all the force of the two ships and drove them down to the beach. The owner wisely followed them, and we paid him his own price and sent him back from the ships well contented with his bargain, and promising to make a market for us the next time we went to his neighbourhood. Catching the bullocks was great fun. We kept a large semicircle with fixed bayonets inclosing the herd down on the beach whilst the sailors selected their beasts, seized them first by the tail, as the most apparent handle, and then by the legs, and flinging them down on the sand tied their legs together; they were then secured by a long rope round the horns, and the legs being untied, were hauled off to the attendant boats.

August 30th.—" Firebrand" arrived and took the "Vesuvius" back to the Admiral. The preparations for the Crimea are being pushed on, and the Admiral writes word that he shall sail in about a week, but that he cannot take me away from this station. To have been neatly put out of the way at Odessa for his own Commander's sake was perhaps fair enough, but it seems hard that I should be passed over a second time. He, of course, wants every vessel with paddle box boats for landing troops, but he must also want every vessel with steam power for towing them across, and I think the "Diamond" might safely be left here whilst the fleet is at Sebastopol to prevent anything coming out.

September 8th.—The first division of the grandest and mightiest expedition ever yet undertaken, not excepting those of the Spanish Armada, hove in sight this morning—it consists of twenty-seven French and Turkish men-of-war, all brimful of troops. The remainder of the expedition has sufficient steam power to be independent of wind, this portion was therefore sent on to a rendezvous oft Fidonisi Island. The "Spitfire" also came this this morning with the welcome news that I was to join the Admiral. I fancy I owe it to Sir Edmund Lyons, who told the Admiral that there should on such an occasion be no "specialities," that all special services should merge in this grand undertaking. There are actually embarked twenty-eight thousand French, and twenty-eight thousand English; a second trip will be made for some of the cavalry which have been left behind. Eupatoria is the spot chosen for landing. It seems a long way from Sebastopol but I suppose the object is to land the troops without opposition, they can then proceed in order of battle to hinder opposition being made to landing the siege train and heavy stores nearer the scene of operations.

The weather is at present very favourable, and although the general opinion is that it is very late in the season, it may turn out that we escape the autumnal fever of the Crimea which is more formidable than even Varna cholera. Captain Spratt, of the "Spitfire," brings us the first news of Bomarsand being taken, and says, "It has given spirit to all our people, some of whom were inclined to think that it was true that the Russians had one hundred and eighty thousand men in the Crimea, and that it was therefore folly to attack them with fifty-six thousand." I shall take this letter on board the flagship and leave it for the first opportunity; no doubt I shall then find some of yours. Mary writes word of a huge box of strawberry jam that has arrived. Many thanks, I shall be well off in that line; wife supplies apricot and mulberry, and sister, strawberry jam.

*LETTER No. 9—Continued.*

At Sea, with Expeditionary Force

bound to Crimea,

September 9th, 1854.

A journal letter will now be of some interest, one day will probably feed it better than one month has hitherto done. On the 7th I had anchored at the southern mouth of the Danube to buy stock, and whilst the boat was on shore saw a fleet to seaward. I recalled the boat, of course, and stood out and found the fleet to consist only of French and Turkish men-of-war, full of troops, but without steamers. I went on board the flagship and heard that having few steamers they thought it better to start as soon as they were ready, leaving the transports with provisions, etc., to follow. The wind was then from the southward, and the French were but fifteen miles south of the Island of Fidonisi, which was the first rendezvous. Admiral Hamelin received news from a small steamer (whilst I was on board) that Admiral Dundas would leave that morning, and said to me, "I shall anchor under Fidonisi Island, or perhaps heave to—what do you think?" I replied, "How do the Turks manage their vessels? If they are not likely to run foul of you, when hove to, I should think you would save time by doing so." Accordingly the fleet was hove to, but during the night the wind veered gradually round, and instead of drifting fifteen miles to the northward, as might fairly have been expected, they drifted fifteen miles to the southward, and when on the 8th the English fleet hove in sight there they were thirty miles to leeward of the rendezvous. I don't think my advice was wrong, for it was given when the wind was south, and when it changed to north the fleet should have made sail.

I think I have before told you that Admirals Dundas and Hamelin are said to be much against this expedition, and so are two-thirds of the bigwigs, both soldiers and sailors. Admiral Bruat (French), Lord Raglan, and Admiral Lyons are the only energetic promoters of it. The consequence of this lukewarmness, or backwardness, is that each of the two Admirals, having urgent orders to prosecute the business and yet strong private personal opinions against it, would be glad to put the blame of any delay at the door of the other, and it seems the English blame the French for this thirty miles loss. No doubt the French have not steamers enough, and are much to be blamed on that account, because three weeks ago they sent for the English Admirals and produced a written agreement, or convention, relative to the method in which this expedition as far as the navies are concerned was to be carried out. In that agreement it was expressly stipulated that every vessel should be towed, and they have failed to carry out that part of the plan.

September 13th.—Six days since the English left Baljik. Here we are at Eupatoria, and I suppose to-morrow the troops, fifty-six thousand strong, with a hundred and fifty field pieces, will disembark. I have had Admiral Lyons on board here for six or seven hours, and he did not hesitate at telling me of all the divisions at the council table; they certainly don't seem at all unanimous, and it is a great pity Admiral Dundas does not go to England and leave Sir Edmund Lyons the Commander-in-chief. We are at this moment anchored three or four miles from the point of disembarkation, and no one but Admiral Dundas can say why we are not in our proper position for landing, since there are still two hours daylight before us now whilst I am writing. The sight of the fleet at sea is very inspiriting. They sail (I speak of the English alone) in seven lines, every vessel being towed by a steamer, or to speak more correctly, every two or three vessels, according to their size, being towed by one steamer. The mass is very imposing. I heard one of the Engineers say the other day that the smoke was for all the world like Staffordshire. Almost all the evidence we have tends to show that forty-five thousand men is the force of the Russians in the Crimea, but it is said that forty thousand more have left Odessa to reinforce them.

There is a hail from the "Agamemnon" to close letter bag, and I must say good-bye to you all for the present. Sir Edmund Lyons has the disembarkation under his orders. Commander Powell commands one-half of the beach, Commander Heath the other; the whole being under Captain Dacres. We don't expect any opposition, the points chosen being, as you will see in the map, a few miles South of Eupatoria, backed by a lake, so that you have but to secure the flanks and your landing goes on unimpeded.

*Statement of Troops, etc., landed at Old Fort between the 14th and 18th September, 1854.*

| | |
|---|---:|
| Light Division, rank and file | 5,454 |
| First ,, ,, ,, | 4,711 |
| Second ,, ,, ,, | 4,222 |
| Third ,, ,, ,, | 3,794 |
| Fourth ,, ,, ,, | 4,367 |
| Artillery ,, ,, | 2,500 |
| Engineers ,, ,, | 379 |
| Cavalry ,, ,, | 1,190 |
| Officers and Sergeants | 2,000 |
| | 28,617 |
| Field Guns | 54 |
| Total Horses, including those for baggage and spare ammunition | 4,000 |

*LETTER No. 10.*

Finished off the River Alma,

September 22nd, 1854.

I have been too busy lately to write my journal up daily, but on the other hand events are of so exciting a nature that they are tolerably well impressed on one's memory. I told you—although not in a journal letter—of our anchoring at Eupatoria on the 13th September, much to every one's astonishment, for we had daylight enough before us to have gone on at once to our intended ground. In the evening I was sent for to the "Agamemnon" where Sir Edmund Lyons told me he had persuaded Admiral Dundas to allow the transports to weigh at one o'clock in the morning so as to be at the intended disembarking point at early daylight, and that I was to go round and distribute the orders. I assured him that if all weighed at once they would infallibly run foul of one another, and persuaded him to allow them to weigh in divisions at one, two, and three o'clock respectively. Thereupon Mends the Flag Captain, Cleeve the Secretary, with myself, set to work tearing sheets of note paper in half and writing out the orders for each ship; Sir Edmund signing as fast as we finished them. It took me until eleven o'clock distributing my share of the orders, and at two in the morning of the 14th a wretched fellow ran on shore close to me and I, of course, had to help him off, which took me until nine, when every one was off, and I was afraid of being out of all the disembarking work. The "Tribune" and "Leander" remained with us for protection in case there should have been any field pieces in the neighbourhood, and as a reward I towed the "Leander" to the fleet, "Tribune" towing the transport.

We arrived just when the boats had landed the first time, and having been appointed to command one half of the beach, I landed at once and remained there until nine o'clock at night, when there were no more unloaded boats and when the signal had been made to annul landing. Unfortunately four or five extra zealous officers attempted to land after that, and the swell having set in heavily, the boats were swamped and left on the beach. There was no opposition whatever made by the Russians to our landing. In fact not a soldier was to be seen, and owing to the excellent arrangements made beforehand, in providing small steam tugs and large double boats with platforms over them, the whole of the infantry and about a dozen guns were landed that day; a much greater achievement than those

who have never seen it can imagine. The next morning the surf was too bad to attempt landing, and we were on the point of returning to Eupatoria, when the swell went down a little and encouraged us to go on. The work went on in the same manner next day, beginning at three in the morning and ending at eight in the evening. By noon of the 18th everything was landed, and then began what must happen more or less in such extensive undertakings, viz., undoing what had been done. The army found they had not pack horses enough, and we had to re-embark the tents; then, after long discussion, they had fully decided to leave the packs and their contents on board and to carry a blanket, a great coat, a shirt, pair of shoes, towel, and the traditional bit of soap, and no more, and all the troops had been landed with this allowance on their backs, but further experience proved that these things would be more easily carried in their knapsacks, which were therefore sent for, but there was some confusion about them owing to this change of view, and many knapsacks were not recovered until the transports had reached Balaklava. The inhabitants are most favourably disposed towards us, and we pay rigorously for everything we get.

The armies advanced on the morning of the 19th, the French being on the right, next to the beach, then the Turks, and then the English; the men-of-war and the commissariat transports following, or rather keeping abreast of the French. Several empty transports were started off for reinforcements to Varna. The bank of the river Alma was the position on which it was intended to encamp, and on approaching it the Russians were discovered in great force and in a strong position ready to dispute the passage. They made a reconnaissance near a small stream called the Bulganak with a large body of cavalry and some guns. A few rounds were fired on each side and then both parties stood fast for the night, the fleets anchoring, with the steamers close in to the mouth of the river.

September 20th. — Daylight showed us both armies as on the previous evening, the Russians in a strong position on the left bank of the Alma, about two and a half or three miles from its mouth out of reach of our guns, and the Allies, two miles from the right bank. A letter from one of the Generals informed us of the plan of attack, which was that the French, fording the mouth of the river, were to endeavour to turn the enemy's left, the Turks were to advance in front (but I have since found that the Turks were left in reserve), and the English to march well up the river and, crossing it, turn the Russian right. Their march was a long one, I should suppose not much less than ten miles, and the French began, I think, too soon. They marched close along the beach and meeting no opposition scrambled up very prettily

## THE BATTLE OF ALMA.

in loose order to the top of the range of hills forming the left bank of the river, their artillery getting up unmolested by a broader road. Their object then evidently was to hold that ground until we came up, and although there was a good deal of firing, of which, on account of the brow of the hill, we could only see the smoke, I don't think they were seriously attacked. I thought I counted fifty-four Russian guns. About two hours after the French had gained their position, the head of our army appeared on the south bank of the river, marching down, as I thought, from inland.

The Russians had, I think, guessed the nature of our plan, and had hitherto confined themselves almost entirely to firing their artillery, keeping their infantry perfectly stationary in six dense close columns, looking like solid squares of, I should suppose, five thousand men each. Their leading battery was placed in an earthwork, and in rear of this earthwork were the remaining guns and these masses of infantry. Our leading regiment, or perhaps it was the second or third (for I think one or two had passed in front of the Russians towards the French) turned to its left to storm the earthwork, the guns in which were quickly limbered up and retired, and one of the Russian masses took the place of the guns in the redoubt. The struggle was fearful and lasted, I suppose, ten minutes; our regiments advancing and firing in line. The Russians did not deploy but gave way whilst still in their solid formation and ran off, beginning at the rear of the mass. The streaming away from the rear was a curious sight. It began with a few individuals, but the numbers increased every minute, until the formation became exactly like a rocket, or a comet with a bushy tail. No doubt those in the rear suffered from our fire as much as those in front, but they had not the excitement of firing at us in return, and thus lost heart more quickly. We were then left in possession of the earthwork, when down came a second mass which was repulsed with the same success, but I think this time the French on the right helped in repulsing them; and there was an end of the battle, as far as we could see, for the Russians went off towards Sebastopol as hard as they could. If the Russian masses had met less valiant men they would have separated the English and French and gained the day. I think that should have been their plan, and if they had turned their whole force against the French at first, instead of doggedly remaining in their original position to carry out their original plan, I believe they would have had every chance of success.

I saw all that I have described to you from the "Niger's" main-top, where I spent four anxious hours. I suppose few people have ever been so well placed for seeing a battle as we were (except on the French side which was hidden from us by the cliff). All the fighting took place within

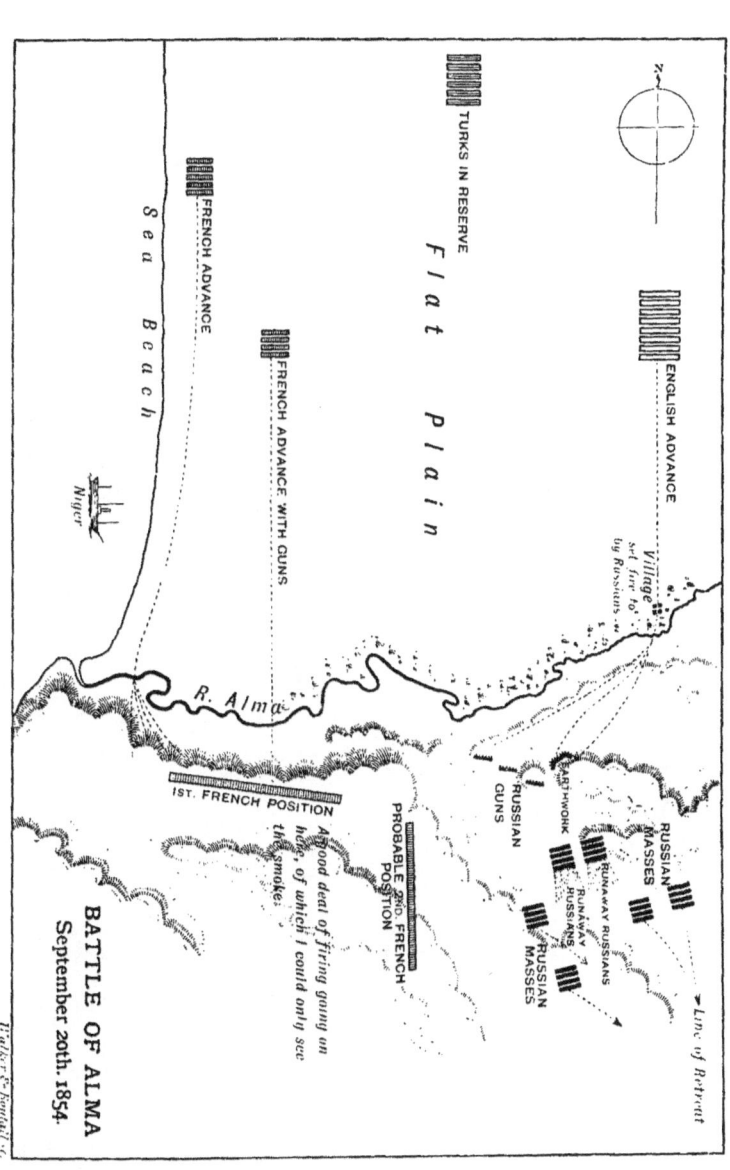

## NATIONAL PECULIARITIES IN FIGHTING.

three miles of us, which from such an elevation, with our good telescopes, is near enough to see everything except such details as were hidden by the inequalities of the ground. The weather was, however, very hazy and there was much smoke, not only from the firing but from a village on the right side of the river to which the Russians had set fire, and I daresay my account is not rigidly accurate. The national peculiarities in the fighting line were very strongly marked; the French climbed their cliff in loose skirmishing order, the English attacked in lines, and the Russians fought in regular Macedonian phalanxes. In the rough plan which I send you I don't attempt to give any idea of numbers, only of positions, and you must remember that the valley in which the Russian army was principally stationed slopes from its head down towards the river's bank. The borders of the river are lined with trees and bushes, in which a good deal of of skirmishing took place. Our army remained for the night in the valley where the Russians had been, pretty well tired I should think, poor fellows! I shall most likely hear more details to-morrow, but want to keep my letter in a forward state, as I suppose despatches will then be sent off.

September 21st.—I have walked round the field of battle and a horrid sight I have seen, but it has often been described and I shall not repeat the description. On actually going over the ground and making inquiries on the spot I find my description of the English advance must be modified; instead of turning the right flank they took the bull by the horns, Lord Gough fashion, and marched straight up to the batteries; the result of which is a loss of about four hundred killed and one thousand five hundred wounded. Some accounts say that owing to the smoke of a village, which the Russians set on fire, the batteries were not seen until it was too late to hesitate; others say that the river was not fordable higher up. I believe the first version the correct one.

September 22nd.—The army has not yet advanced because we have not been able to get the wounded on board; we, that is, the seamen of the fleet, have been working hard all yesterday and to-day carrying them down to the boats in hammocks slung upon oars. The English are now (8 p.m.) all embarked, but there are still many Russians to bring down to-morrow. Their loss is variously estimated at from three thousand to five thousand men, but they must, I think, have carried off some of their officers, as the proportion we have found is small. The only unwounded man we have caught is a General; he is a burly, coarse-looking man, speaking no language but his own.

There seems plenty of enthusiasm amongst our people, and they think having licked the whole

Sebastopol army in the field they will soon get into their stronghold. I believe a division will be landed at Kaffa to prevent reinforcements coming from Anapa or other fortresses near Kertch. Simferopol will also be occupied, as it commands most of the roads, and I suppose if we don't do our work before winter sets in the troops will very likely spend their Christmas there (that is, at Simferopol), unless we get materials for building huts. Of this, however, I know nothing, and perhaps if our works are much advanced it would not do to leave them. The weather as yet has been perfect, and had the expedition been undertaken in July or August we should, I think, have lost more men from the sun than we did at Alma from the enemy. We never could have got through the disembarkation as we did, had the sun been hotter.

There is still a little cholera hanging about, but the "Niger" remains perfectly healthy. My friends prophesy my promotion for the beach work, but I am not sanguine, for I see but few have gained a step for Bomarsund. The feud between the energetic Sir Edmund Lyons and his Commander-in-chief is getting strongly developed. I think Sir Edmund complains rather too bitterly, but no doubt Admiral Dundas is too old for this sort of work, and does not help Sir Edmund as he ought. While Sir Edmund's squadron are slaving like horses the big ships are lying almost idle, three miles off. If they were blockading Sebastopol one would not care, but the port is left quite open and we don't know that they are not sneaking their steamers off to Nicolaev all this time. The army advances to-morrow; we hear the next river is not defended.

[P.S. If you will send me out a couple of sheets of postage stamps I shall be able to prepay.

*LETTER No. 11.*

Finished, Balaklava,
September 28th, 1854.

My last described the battle of Alma, a battle in which British soldiers proved that these are not degenerate days, but that the red coats of this generation cover as bold hearts as those which beat in the last. I have a copy of the official list of killed and wounded, which gives a more favourable account than the estimate I sent you in Letter No. 10: I send you a copy:—

| | |
|---|---:|
| Officers killed | 26 |
| Sergeants killed | 19 |
| Drummers killed | 2 |
| Rank and file killed | 306 |
| Total killed | 353 |
| Officers wounded | 73 |
| Sergeants wounded | 95 |
| Drummers wounded | 17 |
| Rank and file wounded | 1,427 |
| Total wounded | 1,612 |

We cannot get at the French account. To carry down one thousand four hundred and twenty-seven wounded, and two hundred or three hundred sick, a distance of two and a half miles is no joke. We landed a large body of men with hammocks slung upon oars, and brought them down in tolerable comfort, and as fast as a vessel was filled she started off to Constantinople.

The army could not of course move whilst all this was going on, and it was the 23rd before they advanced to their next encampment—the river Katchka, or Kara, as it is named in some of the charts. We have heard from a Russian deserter that they had moored five or six line of battle ships across the harbour's mouth and intended to sink them as soon as the Allied Fleet weighed their anchors, and sure enough directly we weighed, the "Highflyer," which was steaming down in that direction, saw one of them retire from active service. On the 24th the Allies, with three days' provisions on their backs, commenced a forced march, rounding the head of Sebastopol Harbour, and arrived within four miles of Balaklava before they halted. Whilst *en route* they came up with the rearguard of a large body of Russians marching from Sebastopol towards Simferopol, where Menchikoff expects twenty thousand men to arrive from the northward. The Scots Greys, who had only landed the day before, captured a quantity of luggage, killed about thirty men and took about forty prisoners; but Lord Raglan would not allow himself to be diverted from his main object, and prevented all pursuit. Amongst the luggage was Menchikoff's champagne and a boar's head, prepared, it is supposed, for his dinner, of which our hungry staff officers seem to have partaken with double glee. The next morning two divisions marched on Balaklava whilst Sir E. Lyons and his squadron stood off its mouth. Having but a hundred men in garrison it surrendered in a few minutes, and, losing no time, Sir Edmund sent me in to anchor each vessel as she came in, that no space might be lost, and he came in himself in the great "Agamemnon" the next day. Transports, both French and English came tumbling in, and the harbour is now almost as full as it will hold. It is a very small but very snug harbour and its acquisition is of the utmost importance.

Every one is delighted with this march round to the southward of Sebastopol. The army say the position can be held against double its numbers: then it secures our landing stores, provisions, reinforcements, etc., whenever they are wanted; and last, not least, it has stumped the Russians most completely, for all their energies for the last few months have been devoted to strengthening the northern face and they don't seem to have contemplated an attack from this side. We are now busy landing the siege train as hard as we can. There is, at this season, a good road from here to the position chosen, and I suppose in two days more they will all be advanced up to it, and in another week the gabions, etc., of which there is a large store on board the transports, will be all up there too and the grand work ready for beginning.

The weather is still fine, but it is time the troops had their tents to sleep under, for they have now been in open air from the day they landed, and they have had a good deal of hardship to go through and cholera is still at work amongst them. Marshall St. Arnaud is dangerously ill, and has given up command to Canrobert, who is said to be a better man. I have picked up a sick officer here who turns out to be a neighbour of the John Arbuthnots—Major Blane by name. We had an alarm this afternoon, the 28th September, that the Russians were marching in force to attack us, but it turns out to be nothing. We should be a fine prize for them; there are at least thirty vessels in here and so closely packed as to make it difficult to get them out. I intend to set up for harbour master somewhere after this. Of the party of "Nigers" who landed to carry down the wounded two have died of cholera, a third recovered, and I hope it is now all gone.

## LETTER No. 12.

Finished at Balaklava,

October 3rd, 1854.

My letter book tells me I have sent no journal since No. 11 from the Alma, but I think that must be a mistake; nevertheless I number this letter 12, but shall give you a general idea of what has been done since the Alma, for fear the letter book should speak truth. Carrying wounded down from the field of battle was hard work for the seamen and marines, and occupied nearly three days, after which the army advanced and crossed the Katchka, or Kara, as it is in your maps. They were then three miles or less from Fort Constantine, or more correctly the Star Fort — Fort Constantine being the proper name of the one at the mouth of the harbour. A forced march was then taken round the head of Sebastopol harbour to a position four miles from Balaklava, into which place a division marched the next day; the "Agamemnon," "Sanspareil," "Highflyer," "Diamond," and "Niger," coming off the harbour's mouth at the same time. Sir Edmund sent me in immediately with directions to anchor well up the harbour in order to leave room for the "Agamemnon," and added, "I shall send a few small ships in; make them anchor out of the way." However, I had no sooner got in than I found them tumbling in as fast as possible; fortunately I had begun from the beginning to pack them much as you may see them off London Bridge, only with their bows across the river and their sterns secured to the shore, and was able to squeeze in all that came. The "Agamemnon" came in the next day, and we have all been working hard ever since, clearing transports of every sort but more especially those laden with the siege guns.

I am writing on the 2nd October. We have now landed all the guns except two, and the artillery have taken them all up to the camp, which is now close round the south side of Sebastopol. Carts, waggons, camels, and everything available, are now in constant requisition for the conveyance of shot, shell, and powder. Those French are funny fellows! It so happened that the only guns taken at the Alma were taken by our soldiers, who stormed the earthwork battery; the next day six artillery horses and a limber under charge of a French corporal came down, and he was about to walk off with one of them, but was fortunately stopped by some English officers. The man said he had been sent to measure the gun!—a process which certainly would have been more easily gone

## ST. ARNAUD'S SUCCESSOR.

through with compasses and tape than with six horses and a limber. There were a few small mortars at Balaklava, a shell from one of which burst very near Lord Raglan (for the garrison here made a show of resistance) at the taking of the place. There was not at the capture a Frenchman within four miles, but the next day some of them discovered the mortars and had actually got them down from their position to the road before they were stopped, and would in a very short time have embarked them as trophies with St. Arnaud's luggage. Canrobert, St. Arnaud's successor is much more highly spoken of than the latter was, and although I have not heard of any serious disagreement between the two former chiefs, the two present ones are likely to agree still better. I am afraid Sir Edmund Lyons and Admiral Dundas don't get on very well together; the latter is rather old for his position and does not understand the extraordinary energy and impetuous nature of the former.

October 3rd.—Yesterday a naval brigade of one thousand men with fifty ships' guns came in to serve in the front; besides these men we have landed a thousand marines and encamped them on the heights around Balaklava for our own protection, for some of the Sebastopol troops are gone to Bachtchiserai and are there awaiting reinforcements from the north. A direct route runs from Bachtchiserai to Balaklava, and it would be worth a good deal to the Russians to take this place, even for one hour. The harbour contains, amongst other valuable siege material, five hundred tons of gunpowder; so that one shell might make fine havoc. An expedition is just starting for Yalta, a place forty miles or so east of this, where there are large wine stores. We are to take the wine *vi et armis* for the use of the French troops, and I think the object of English ships forming part of the expedition must be to see that the French really do pay for what they take.

We do not expect to begin the trenches until the 6th, as Lord Raglan does not wish to open his fire until he can bring it to bear in heavy force. I am afraid it will take eight or ten days to get the ships' guns up, and he would hardly wait so long as that. The French were at first a little jealous of our putting so many ships into this harbour, though they had no reason to be so, for *every ship* of theirs that came to the harbour's mouth was brought in. The result, however, is that they have taken their transports to some very good little harbours between Cheronese and Sebastopol, and on account of this arrangement the positions of the two armies have been changed—the English being now on the right and the French on the left, each of us with our respective ports.

We get but little information from outside, and don't know in the least what force is collecting at Bachtchiserai. And I believe we don't much care;

Sebastopol is our object, that once in our hands I suppose we shall attend to our friends in its neighbourhood. The weather is still beautiful and we have had no more cholera. The health of the troops is very fair and improving daily. They have at last got a portion of tents given them— I wish they had them all, for it is very cold at night.

*LETTER No. 13.*

Finished, Balaklava,

October 8th, 1854.

On the afternoon of the 3rd October I got upon Major Blane's horse and rode to the camp to look at Sebastopol. I was perfectly astonished at the extent of the works which the Russians have thrown up in the last week. The only thing worthy of the name of a fortification on this side of the harbour, before the arrival of our army, was a stone martello tower on our extreme right—that is to say, at the upper end of Sebastopol harbour, and there was, besides this, a miserable looking loopholed wall enclosing the sea face of the town. Since our appearance they are said to have had two thousand men continuously at work, and they have enclosed the ground between the two permanent works of which I have spoken with an earthwork fortification, having regular curtains and bastions and in some places (but I cannot positively say as to all) ditches. The guns are not yet all mounted in these works, but some half a dozen or so are, and they play continuously upon our

## GETTING READY FOR ACTION.

lines. They must be of very heavy calibre, for the Engineers measured with sextants the distance at which one of the shot struck from its gun, and found it to be four thousand yards. Our troops are spread along the whole south side of Sebastopol within about a mile and a half, or less, of the town. The enemy's shell appear to be nearly harmless, for no aim can be taken with such high elevations. I have only heard of two men being killed as yet, but I should have thought we would have been as well a little further off.

The thing that strikes all of *us* most is that we should allow the Russians to build these works and mount their guns without the slightest attempt to check or annoy them. It seems so clear that a man who is unmolested can heap up many more shovels full of earth in a day than a man who is looking round every five minutes to know where the shell burst, and whether it touched any of his friends or came near himself, that I should have thought we ought to have established a few stray guns in batteries at once, without waiting for the whole force to be ready for simultaneous opening. It is said that Lord Raglan and Sir J. Burgoyne do not intend to fire until they can bring an overwhelming force of guns to bear, and that the latter says it will then take but twenty-four hours to destroy all he sees.

October 6th.—I believe I mentioned before the arrival of a thousand men from the fleet with fifty 32-Pr guns; these are now reinforced by the "Beagle's" two long Lancaster guns of 95 cwt., also by two equally heavy guns from the "Terrible" on the common principle. Great efforts are being made to get these up. Hore, who commands the "Beagle," goes up with the brigade, being attached to Lord Raglan's staff in some temporary manner, and so I hope he will come in for promotion when the grand event takes place. The shell for these Lancaster guns are at present all made by hand, the ordinary shells cost £20 a piece and some extraordinary ones cost, I am told, £100 each.

October 7th.—The Russians seem to be wondering what we are about, for yesterday they made a strong reconnaissance towards our lines and this morning a large body of infantry and cavalry came down in the direction of this harbour. Our horse artillery sent them off in double quick time. Sir Edmund Lyons has been doing all he can (without success hitherto) to get a few batteries run up here, which would make the place very strong. This morning's reconnaissance has done more than all his talking, and the Engineers are now actually at work at them. Carrying guns with all their shot, shell, and ammunition, is heavier work than people seem to have anticipated. The day now named for beginning the trenches is the 10th. The joint expedition of French and English steamers to Yalta, with the view of getting wine for the French army, has just returned; they found none, and so we shall get the discredit of being pirates without the solid advantages of the trade. I believe we joined the expedition in order to make sure of the French paying for what they took; they only intended to pay in *bons de trésor*, and when they heard we had £10,000 in gold they said it was *un grand malheur*. It seems generally understood that the new French Commander-in-Chief is a much better General than his predecessor. I am glad to say, that the line of battle ships will be brought in to help at the grand cannonade. It would be a shameful thing if they were merely to look on when there was a possibility of making the slightest diversion in favour of the heroes of Alma, who will, I suspect, have hot work of it. Sir Edmund Lyons will leave this harbour soon, and I hope to accompany him. There will be a little tustling as to who is to remain, but I think it will be Tatham, and that we, Sir Edmund's special squadron, will go out with him. It is but fair that having had all the work we should also have the fighting, from which the rewards of promotion will accrue. I am, when I have time to think of such things, inclined to speculate on being promoted for the disembarkation, which would leave C.B. open to me for the capture. Nothing like a few castles in the air! I have good accounts of Mary up to the 25th. An artillery officer has just been breakfasting with me who had a son born to him during the battle of Alma.—No more cholera on board.

## LETTER No. 14.

Finished, Balaklava,

October 13th, 1854.

October 9th.—I will try and keep my journal going with a little more regularity than I have hitherto done. It was blowing so hard to-day that no ships could come in or go out in safety, so that my special services would not be required, and I took a holiday and walked out to the lines with Moore and a Captain Twopenny, who was some months ago reporter to *The Times*. He has since been living on board various men-of-war, as a private friend of the respective Captains, and is at present on board the "Highflyer." We walked out to the extreme right, and found a battery built for the reception of three of our heavy naval guns, placed so as to be three thousand yards from two line of battle ships and one steamer, the guns from which impede our approaches. I should not have guessed the distance to be quite so much, but I suppose it has been measured with sextants. I see that, from experiments made from the "Excellent" at an old line of battle ship, the number of shot which may be expected to hit at that distance is only eleven or twelve per cent. and so I am afraid the battery, which will probably open to-morrow morning, will not sink the ships as soon as is expected. This battery appears not as yet to have been discovered by the Russians, and our sentries made us sneak up to it, stooping down so as not to be seen and not to draw a fire upon it. We had a good look at the ships and harbour from behind it, and then sneaked to a pile of stones on the left, whence I saw a body of Russian skirmishers lying down within a thousand yards of us, but their attention was evidently turned on something to our left. We then went back to the guard, which was a little in the rear supporting the working party in the battery, and found that these Russian skirmishers had been seen by their outlying sentries and in addition a column of infantry, and that a message had been sent in to the camp, and the troops were all placed under arms in front of their respective encampments. Presently the Colonel of the guard came up, and then Sir Colin Campbell, and then an aide-de-camp from Sir G. Browne, to know what was going on. By this time we could see that large bodies of French and Russians were out on the left, and in Sir Colin's opinion the Russians were making a reconnaissance. I suppose some of our troops must have been seen by the Russians, for a fire of shot and shell just then commenced in our direction, and at the same time a good deal of firing took place on the French, but no musketry was interchanged, and I believe nothing more occurred. We were obliged to come away to save our daylight in. The Russians must have fired by this time upwards of five hundred shot or shell, and the result has been two men killed!

October 11th.—Moore explained to us at dinner yesterday why so few are killed. His explanation is that a man may be considered as exposing a surface of eight square feet, and that when standing at a distance even of six feet from a shell about to burst into (we will say ten pieces) the chances of being struck are as eight to one-tenth of the surface of a sphere (in square feet) of six feet radius, which comes to about seven to one in favour of escaping—a most consolatory piece of mathematics.

We began in earnest upon our entrenchments yesterday, two thousand men were at work all night, and I understand great progress has been made. The French position is better than ours, their battery will be within nine hundred yards of the Russians, ours one thousand two hundred. We are obliged to put our guns on the crests of hills, as there is no intention of making the zig-zag approaches which are made against a regular fortress; this difference of distance therefore only means that the nearest hill at our end happens to be one thousand two hundred yards from the enemy, whilst that at the French end is nine hundred. It is a very suitable arrangement for us, as our guns are considerably heavier than theirs. We have various reports relative to the danger of Balaklava; one that the Greeks intend to set fire to the town and burn all our stores. This has been met by ordering all the male inhabitants to quit, which may sound harsh to your ears, but you must remember the great interests which are at stake, and that we are bound to take every possible precaution. Another report is that the Russians intend to attack us here by way of a diversion from Sebastopol; that will be met by some very pretty little batteries we are throwing up and by three thousand Turks and one thousand marines.

October 13th.—I paid another visit to the camp yesterday; the distance is a good seven miles, and the road itself is very interesting. It is covered with conveyances of all sorts—Crimean bullock or camel waggons, Turkish bullock waggons brought from Varna, Maltese mule carts from Malta, all with provisions, etc., and artillery waggons with shot, shell, or fascines and gabions; then comes an occasional aide-de-camp at a gallop, or an infantry officer, dusty and weary-looking, returning from Balaklava laden with whatever he has been able to buy—some preserved meats or a bottle of brandy, perhaps three or four ducks, or a pound of candles! He looks quite triumphant as he passes you with his prize. You can have no idea of the appearance of a campaigning soldier if you have only seen them in St. James's Park or in a garrison ball-room. They live in their full dress coats, and the consequence is the scarlet has turned to port wine colour, and the gold lace and epaulettes to a dark coppery colour; the coat is generally full of holes, and the individual wears no shirt. The change of life to them must be very great, and some of them feel it a good deal. It is supposed now that we shall open fire with about one hundred guns on the 15th. Time flies, and I should like to see a beginning.

The weather is still fine but we had two very cold days a week ago. We are all well and have no more cholera. Last news of Mary, September 27th—very well. You should send us reinforcements, if you have any. Our position is very strong, but no doubt we shall soon be considerably outnumbered.

*LETTER No. 15.*

Finished, Katcha River,

October 18th, 1854.

October 16th. — "The batteries will open to-morrow" has so long been the "latest news from the camp" that we begin to doubt if they will ever open at all. But there does seem really to be some chance of it now, for the "Agamemnon" left Balaklava for the fleet yesterday, leaving word for us all to follow. I did not leave until this morning as I was coaling, which is rather satisfactory, for when quite full of coals the engine and boilers are very well protected from shot. On arriving I called on Admiral Dundas, and found that at a consultation of the allied Admirals it had been determined that a sea attack should be made on the batteries. But as a man-of-war only carries eighty rounds of shot for each gun, or a hundred and sixty for one broadside, and as a portion has been landed with the fifty naval guns, they only muster on an average about a hundred and forty rounds each, which would or could all be fired away in a day. So that the particular day on which the fleet is to be brought into play remains to be determined on by the Generals. The day of assault will probably be *the* day.

I brought with me as passenger the surgeon of the flagship, who has for the last fortnight been attached to the naval brigade. He gives a bad account of the sanitary state of the army, and still worse of the want of organisation of the Army Medical Staff this and the commissariat are still loudly complained of. I know one glaring instance myself. There is, at Balaklava, a transport appropriated for the reception of sick officers, but instead of appointing a regular doctor to her they have made some arrangement that the doctor of the regiment on guard or of some shifting body shall visit the ship once a day (or it may be more often); it is proverbial that doctors differ, and the consequence of this arrangement is that a sick man may each day be treated in a different manner, for no record of the case and its treatment is ever left.

October 17th.—Last night at 9 o'clock a letter from Lord Raglan to the Admiral arrived, requesting that the fleets should commence their work to-day. Conferences between the allied Admirals took place, and this morning all the Captains assembled on board the Flagship for discussion and agreement as to the plan to be pursued. We were told that when the Admirals had first agreed to offer the services of the fleets to the Generals it was arranged (and the document signed by them all was shown us) that the French should attack the batteries on the south side of the harbour and the English those on the north, and that a

## THE COMBINED FLEETS IN ACTION. 83

line drawn right down Sebastopol harbour should separate the two fleets. Our plan, therefore, was to put our steamers on the starbord side of the line of battle ships, and to tow down the north shore and anchor in our stations. But, according to Admiral Dundas's statement, Admiral Hamelin had just been on board and proposed that he, Admiral Dundas, should sweep round to the southward, and then bring his ships up in succession, forming on the French van, and thus continuing the line as far on as it might reach, and Admiral Dundas foolishly agreed to this, giving us to understand that if he had not consented the French would have refused to engage the batteries at all. All the Captains said, "You agreed to leave the south side to the French, and not to anchor south of a certain line; surely you may bring your own ships into action in the way you think best."

It was ultimately settled that "Agamemnon," "Sanspareil," and "London" (to which ship the "Niger" was lashed on the off-shore side) should go down according to the original plan; that the "Albion" should pay special attention to the Wasp Fort; and the remainder of the ships should follow the French plan. This separation of our ships, and a general order issued by Admiral Dundas, to the effect that every one was to do as he pleased, caused our ships to be placed in a very irregular manner. However, our three got into action at half-past one, or so, and the "Albion" shortly afterwards; but those which swept round did not come into play until very late. Our fire was directed at Fort Constantine, and was continued about an hour-and-a-half very well and steadily. By that time the "Albion" had been set on fire and so knocked about by the Wasp Fort and some neighbouring guns that she was obliged to leave it, and the Wasp then began to sting us, so that Captain Eden directed me to steam on, and took his ship out of fire. We were shortly afterwards recalled by the "Agamemnon," but by the time we got back "Bellerophon" and "Queen" had taken our place, and there was such a crowd of ships and so much smoke that we could only get an occasional shot. Finding that I could only use the "Niger's" long pivot gun, and that the "London" having landed two hundred men with the naval brigade, could not work all her guns, I offered Captain Eden the rest of my ship's company, and Dunn went with them and worked the "London's" upper deck guns. This was rather a good *coup* for him; as I find now, what I did not know then, that the "London's" senior lieutenants being with the naval brigade on shore, Dunn was actually the senior on board in the action; which may, I hope, help him to his promotion. The squadron returned to this anchorage after sunset, but the "Rodney" grounded whilst still under fire, and was with difficulty towed off by the "Spiteful" and "Lynx" without much loss.

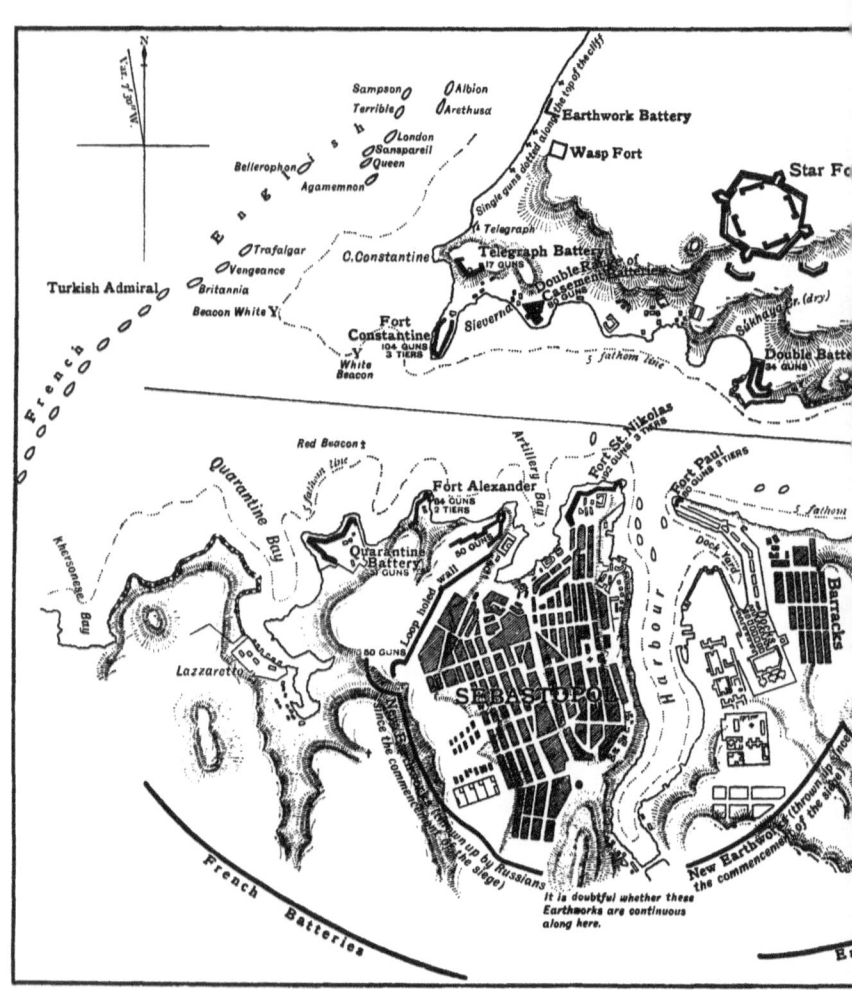

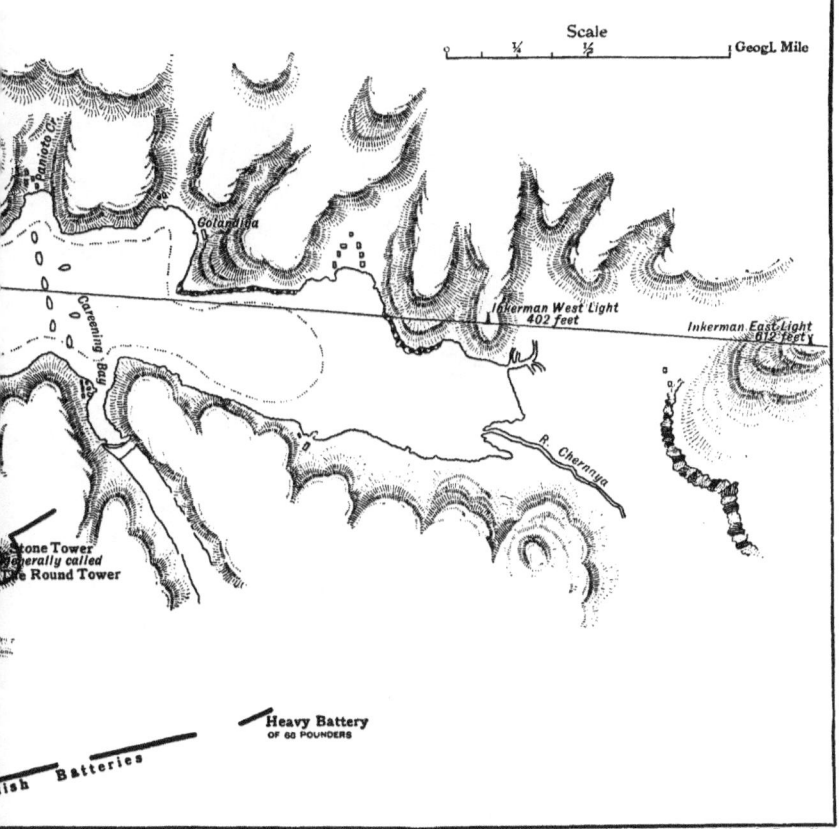

## THE LAURELS OF THE DAY.

In spite of Mr. Oliphant's predictions, I could only make out that we had destroyed two of the Fort Constantine's embrasures. The whole face of it was speckled with shot marks, and, taking the proportion of space covered by an embrasure, I should say four or five shells must have gone into each, and if so they must have lost a large number of men. I spent most of my time on the "London's" poop. I have lost one killed and four slightly wounded; a few ropes were shot through, and two shot struck the hull, in spite of our huge protector. The "London" has four killed and eighteen wounded. The laurels of the day are decidedly due to the "Agamemnon," "Sanspareil," and "Albion." The "Retribution's" mainmast is shot away. We still hear the shore batteries at work, but I don't know how they are getting on. Our three ships were about one thousand six hundred yards from Fort Constantine, the other English I should say a good two thousand; the French still further—much too far to hurt stone walls.

P.S.—I suppose we shall renew the attack on the day of the assault.

*LETTER No. 16.*

Finished, October 23rd, 1854,

Katcha River.

October 20th.—I sent off Letter No. 15 on the morning after the naval attack. I find the total loss is forty-five killed and two hundred and sixty-three wounded, but it must be remembered that "the wounded" includes almost every scratch, so that there are not probably more than a hundred hospital cases amongst the two hundred and sixty-three. Some of the ships were a good deal damaged, the "Albion," "Arethusa," and "Sans-pareil" especially; and the "Agamemnon" has almost all her spars damaged. I believe I mentioned the "Albion" as one of the ships deserving of special notice, but I find I was quite mistaken. It is true that she was brought into action very well, towed by the "Firebrand," Captain Stewart,* and that she suffered the heaviest loss; but I find on an alarm of fire a large portion of the crew rushed on board the "Firebrand," instead of trying their utmost to put the fire out,

---

* Now Admiral Sir Wm. Houston Stewart, G.C.B.

and that they in fact fired very little at the enemy but closed the magazines and left off firing the moment the alarm was given. It must, however, be remembered that her Captain and the best of the lieutenants were with the naval brigade, and it seems that the want of officers was very much felt. We hear better news from the entrenchments to-day. It is said they are gradually subduing the Russian fire, and that our attack, whether it damaged the Russians or no, did at all events raise the spirits of our friends in the camp; and I believe moral effect is in warlike operations of quite as much consequence as physical effect.

They say that the Lancaster gun which was to have done such wonders is all humbug. You may perhaps be aware that it was always known that it shot like an Irish gun, round a corner, and that in the range table supplied with it you are told that at one thousand yards distance you must point so many yards to the left; at two thousand yards so many more, etc., etc. But it turns out that you never can make sure which corner it is going to turn, and if you point carefully fifty yards to the left it is an even bet that it will strike fifty yards to the right of the object aimed at, and that in fact it is most uncertain. This may be an error in the details of the manufacture, and may be corrected by greater experience, and more perfect machinery, but for the present the guns seem to be useless. We are quite idle to-day, but heavy firing is going on in the trenches about six miles from us, and watching with a glass is every one's occupation. They set fire to a large building near the dockyard this afternoon, but it was unfortunately a dead calm and the fire did not spread. Our look out steamer reports that Fort Constantine is being propped up with wooden beams, which looks as if we had seriously damaged it, and the Russians are lining the whole edge of the north cliff with guns, which will make a second naval attack impossible unless we land the previous night and spike those guns. It was the few guns that were there on the 17th which so quickly silenced the "Albion" and "Arethusa," and which, when they were out of the way, induced the "London" to make a prudent retreat; as also the "Bellerophon" and "Queen," which subsequently took up that position for a short time.

October 22nd.—Varying accounts from the camp. I saw the only two letters which reached Admiral Dundas yesterday; one was from Captain Lushington, who commands the naval brigade, and the other from Captain Tatham, who is stationed at Balaklava, and who had just come down from the lines. The former wrote in a most dismal, downhearted strain, the latter in quite a cheerful one; so it is difficult to form any judgment. I hear the French are all quarrelling. The army and navy are anything but united services, and the Engineers and Artillerymen are each abusing the other; the *entente cordiale* does not, however, suffer, but goes on harmoniously. Sir Edmund Lyons returned yesterday evening from a conference, and reports that a Russian sortie was made the night before last and succeeded in spiking three French mortars, but they were then repulsed and some prisoners taken, one of whom a not unwilling one. A Captain reports his side to have lost five thousand men since the batteries opened their fire; that the garrison are rather in a bad way and getting a little insubordinate; and that Admiral Korniloff (whose luggage I captured off Odessa) and Nachimoff, the "Sinope" hero, are killed.

We have nothing but the ordinary duties of the ship to do, and for a wonder had a quiet Sunday to-day. It was very warm, and so I had service on the upper deck, and was much struck by the extraordinary contrast of our offering up prayers to the "Author of peace and lover of concord," whilst the booming of guns whose shot were dealing death and destruction was loud in our ears. The firing is continuous from six in the morning until six in the evening. At night we hear a gun at about every ten minutes—I suppose a shell thrown from a mortar to prevent the Russians sleeping too soundly. The riflemen are doing good service *à la Bomarsand;* finding cover for themselves somewhere between the rival batteries, and firing at the embrasures directly a gun has been fired, so as to prevent its being reloaded.

October 23rd.—I was this morning suddenly ordered on a court of inquiry, and am now as suddenly ordered to go to Balaklava, with recruits for the naval brigade. I return to-morrow. No news from the camp to-day.

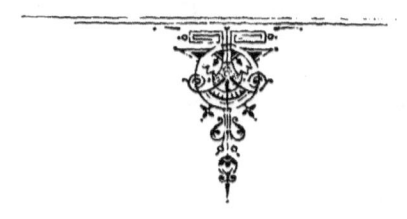

*LETTER No. 17.*

Finished, No. 4 Battery,

Balaklava lines, November 3rd, 1854.

Direct nevertheless H.M.S. " Niger."

October 27th.—Here I am, writing under a tent, having turned soldier for a time; but I had better keep my narrative continuous, and go back to my last date, October 24th. When I was sent to Balaklava with a reinforcement of two hundred seamen for the naval brigade, I took advantage of the opportunity to ride out to the lines. To all appearance matters may go on as at present for a long time; the Russian earthworks are certainly a good deal knocked about, but there are still embrasures, and there are still guns, and I am told that if a gun is dismounted to-day it will be replaced in the night. We have but one advantage over the besieged, which is that all our shot which miss the earthwork go into the town, whereas theirs bound harmlessly away, as our encampment is purposely kept out of gunshot. Our force is not strong enough for completely investing the place, and so they are probably as well supplied as, or better than, we are, excepting in such articles as are brought from seaward.

I returned to the fleet carrying with me a requisition for ammunition, which I took back on the 25th, and on arriving I found that we had met our first reverse. On that morning, at daylight, a large body of Russians had shown themselves opposite a hill in front of the Balaklava position, on which hill we had built some strong redoubts, armed them with heavy guns, and garrisoned them with Turks. These gentlemen did not stand the Russian attack upon the right battery five minutes, but ran away as hard as they could; on seeing which those in the other batteries did not even wait to be attacked, but ran like mad also, leaving altogether seven guns in the Russian hands. About six hundred cavalry then charged the front of our position, and were received and turned in their advance by the 93rd Highlanders in line; our heavy cavalry then charged and completely routed the Russians. So far the Turks had lost our guns, but as far as the English were concerned all had gone well. By this time, however, Lord Raglan had come down and sent an order by Captain Nolan (whose name you may know as having written a book about horses) to Lord Lucan to attack the enemy. Both Lord Lucan and Lord Cardigan said it was madness, but the cavalry have been a good deal taunted with not having yet

## THE CHARGE OF THE LIGHT BRIGADE.

done anything, and Captain Nolan appears to have delivered his message in a taunting manner, and on went the Light Brigade between two fires from guns and masses of infantry besides. They made a splendid charge, killed the Russian gunners at their guns, but lost half their number—something like three hundred are said to have been

killed or wounded. A French General looking on with Lord Raglan's staff from the edge of the plateau, exclaimed: "C'est magnifique, mais ce n'est pas la guerre." The only consolation we have is that, although it is a victory for the Russians, they must have gained with it as wholesome a fear of our cavalry as they gained of our infantry at Alma.

Inspirited, I suppose, by this success, they made a sortie from Sebastopol against Sir de Lacy Evans's division on the 25th and were completely licked; our loss was seven killed and seventy-one wounded, the Russians about five hundred.

November 3rd.—The Russian loss in their sortie is now said to have been one thousand. After the cavalry business it was, I believe, decided to give up Balaclava and contract our front. "Sanspareil" "Tribune," "Sphinx," "Niger," and "Vesuvius" were sent off to help in reimbarking everything, but at, I believe, Sir E. Lyons's urgent remonstrance the plan was abandoned, and the resolution taken to strengthen and hold the position. Instead therefore of helping to load merchant ships we landed a number of marines and seamen. I took command of the former and Powell of the latter; my station being in a battery, with Sir Colin Campbell, in the centre of the valley. Our position is by no means pleasant. We see the Russian army two miles from us, its advanced post is only two thousand six hundred yards off, it is estimated at from twenty to thirty thousand men, whereas we have but three thousand English and two thousand Turks; with, however, four thousand French a mile in our rear, who will come to our aid if attacked. We have entrenched ourselves, and are safe if the Turks stand like good men and true, and if the Russians do not attack at night, when the military opinion is that their numbers would give them much greater advantage than by day.

I have great confidence in Sir Colin Campbell, he has passed his life in the field and is one of our best practical soldiers, and is as cool as can be when an alarm is given, but yet never neglects the slightest precautions nor relaxes the strictest personal vigilance. I have joined his mess. One of his Staff is Colonel Stirling, who knows Douglas a little, being a brother of the "Stirling Club" Stirling; another, a very nice fellow, a son of Sir L. Shadwell; and a young one named Mansfield.

October 30th.—We have now made our entrenchments so good that we feel quite safe by day. Night alarms are frequent and harassing, but one only has proved to have been a real enemy, on which occasion a small body of horse, being challenged by our outside sentry, fired a volley and galloped off. We all sleep in our clothes, and indeed one half of the force sleeps in the trenches, and from the sentry's alarm cry of "Turn out," "Turn out," "Stand to your arms," not many seconds elapse before everyone is on his legs and running to his station.

October 31st.—We were disturbed as usual last night and kept up in the cold from eleven to one; it was not, however, this time an alarm on our side, but on that of the Russians, they suddenly commenced firing both great guns and musketry and kept at it for an hour. We cannot understand it;

for one can hardly suppose them to go on so long firing at nobody, without discovering it—particularly as there was good moonshine all the time. Shortly after daylight this morning five Cossacks came prowling about between the two lines, apparently looking for the killed and wounded enemy! The best of the joke is that General Bosquet, who is near the Russians, had intended when the moon went down to give them an "Alerte" by sending in one company to fire, and run away. He must, however, have forgotten that unless he sends us previous warning an *alerte* for the Russians is also an *alerte* for us, and that we should be quite as much harassed by his amusements as the enemy.

November 3rd.—The two last nights have been passed in peace and quietness, and our ditches are now so deep that we feel quite safe. The Russians came yesterday and made a strong reconnaissance of our extreme right, but after exchanging a few shot retired. My own opinion is (and I hear it is also that of the French Generals) that their position here is not taken up so much with a view to offensive operations against us, as to secure the safe retreat of what remains of the Sebastopol garrison, when the place is taken; which no one doubts it will be sooner or later.

The French have now a heavy battery at work close up to the Russians, and two or three days more will probably see the town entered; but it does not follow then that the north side, nor even that the dockyard, will fall. The French are anxious to have the first attack left to their management, for the streets are all barricaded, and they say " they are more used to that sort of thing than we are." They intend to take the end houses, and work their way slowly and surely through the partitioned walls, thus taking the barricades in flank and working round them. We should get on much faster with thirty thousand more men. We can now neither invest Sebastopol, nor keep off the army, which is now literally besieging the besiegers. The first thing to do after securing the town will be to turn out and lick our neighbour, General Liprandi; then make as much hay as we can in the dockyard, etc., during the little sunshine that remains, and then make ourselves as warm as we can for the winter. This is as much as can reasonably be expected, unless stories told by deserters of distress and insubordination in the garrison should prove to have more truth in them than stories usually have.

*LETTER No. 18.*

Finished at No. 4 Battery,

Balaklava,

November 8th, 1854.

November 5th.—This is the beginning of what we all expect to be a very critical week. A few days ago a soldier deserted to the enemy, and it is supposed gave information as to the hour at which the parties working in our trenches and batteries were relieved; the consequence was that at that hour a tremendous fire opened from all the Russian batteries, which has been continued on every successive morning since, although we, of course, changed our hour on the second day.

This morning we heard the usual cannonade at about the same hour, and attributed it to the same cause; but at broad daylight about 7 a.m. we saw masses of Russian infantry moving along, and as we at first thought threatening our front. It has, however, since turned out that from (so far as I as yet know) the negligence of our people on the right flank of the besieging army, the Russians succeeded in surprising our troops stationed at

## OUR TROOPS SURPRISED.

that part, and there has been fought during the day a most desperate battle, in which we ultimately remain the victors, but at a fearful cost of life on both sides. We depend for our information upon straggling visitors, messengers, etc., from the camp, and it is hardly worth while filling my paper with reports—which may to-morrow be all contradicted—when I know you will receive with my letter many others from "Our Own Correspondents," besides the official reports. Peel came down to Balaklava in the evening—very hoarse—he said he had spent the day "cheering on Her Majesty's Guards." The troops we saw must have amounted to something like twenty thousand; they made a slight cannonading attack on the lines in rear of the Sebastopol army, but soon withdrew, and we go to bed with the pleasant anticipation of a probable attack upon our end of the line to-morrow morning. It is said that Osten Sacken has arrived from Odessa, and that they were his troops which had the fight this morning. "Why have we no reinforcements?" is at the present the question in every one's mouth. Canrobert said to Sir Colin Campbell the other day, "Nous avons pris Balaklava trop facilement, et on pensait que ce serait la même chose avec Sebastopol, mais on se trompe." We hear he intends working his way very slowly and surely into Sebastopol, and if there were no relieving army outside it would no doubt be well to do so, but matters are now changed, and I think a little extra risk should be incurred for the sake of a few days gain in time. I suppose, as it is quite agreed that the French end of Sebastopol is the right one to assault, we shall leave all the arrangements to him.

November 7th.—These are the days for strong contrasts. Yesterday I walked over the field of battle and meditated on the horrors (as such a sight may well be called) of war; to-day I am revelling in the delight of Malta letters announcing my " boy's " birth, and my wife's well doing. My son shows *decided* symptoms of intelligence (this is only for the mothers amongst you). Admiral Stewart and Commander Chamberlain called upon him, and he fixed his eyes on the former and took no notice whatever of the latter! As to his personal appearance I hear he is " a splendid little fellow," but doubtless your own experiences must have taught you that they are always that.

To turn now to affairs of more public interest, I rode yesterday to the camp, and walked over to the battlefield, and talked and had descriptions of the events of the 5th from several of the actors in it. The morning was peculiarly misty and dull, and there is, I fancy, but little doubt that we were more or less surprised, although General Penefather and his Staff (he commands in that quarter) stoutly deny it. The Russians have a more numerous and a heavier artillery than ours, and they had about

## THE BATTLE OF INKERMAN.

thirty-five guns in position, and commenced a cannonade from them, simultaneously with the

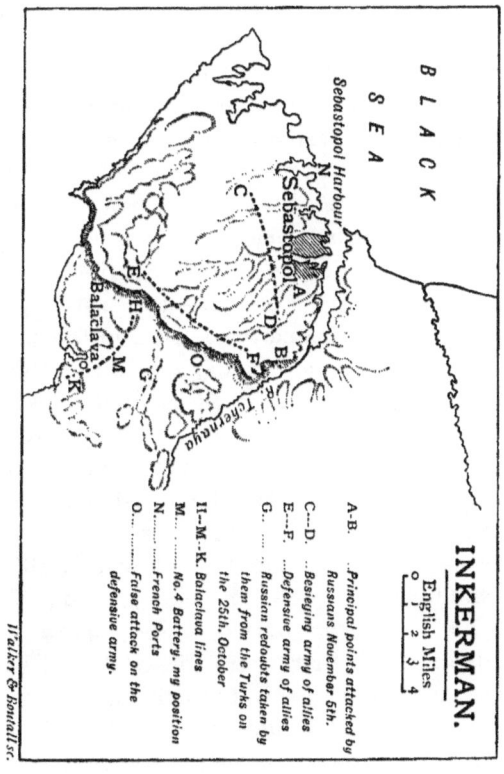

INKERMAN.

A-B. ...Principal points attacked by Russians November 5th.
C---D. ...Besieging army of allies
E---F. ...Defensive army of allies
G. ...... Russian redoubts taken by them from the Turks on the 25th. October
H---M---K. Balaclava lines
M. ......No. 4 Battery, my position
N. ......French Forts
O. ........False attack on the defensive army.

assault by solid masses of infantry up the sides of the hill at A and B.

As fast as one column was driven back, a fresh one rushed up, but only to meet its predecessor's fate; and so the battle went on, a succession of thick massy columns, covered by an enormous artillery fire, rushing up, met by lines of infantry and invariably repulsed. The French sent fifteen thousand men to our assistance, but for them we must have been overpowered by numbers. Sir G. Cathcart, an impetuous chivalric soldier, led his division too far in advance, and paid the penalty in his own death; General Strangways, of the Artillery, was killed; Generals Bentinck, Adams, Buller, and Goldie wounded—the last has since died. The battle lasted from seven in the morning until three in the afternoon, when the Russians returned in good order to Sebastopol. I am told the official returns will show four hundred and forty killed and one thousand seven hundred wounded on our side; on the Russian it must be enormously greater. I went over the most hotly contested portion of the ground, where, although the wounded had been brought in, none of our dead had yet been buried, and I speak within bounds in saying there were fifteen dead Russians to one Englishman; but then many Russians whom I saw dead would probably, had they been English, have been brought in wounded the previous evening. The Russians come on with loud yells and shouts; it is said they were all more or less drunk, and that most of their water bottles had spirits in them. It is said also that they killed our wounded, as they lay helpless on the ground, whenever the ebb and flow of the battle left them the opportunity.

Whilst all this was going on, on the right front, we at Balaklava were alarmed by seeing fifteen or twenty thousand infantry come over the heights at G, apparently to attack us, but they were merely making some change in their front, and went over again out of our sight and made a false attack on the French at O—I see I have mentioned this in the beginning of my letter. In the course of the day a heavy sortie was made against the French left battery, which was repulsed by the French lining the rampart of their battery with infantry, awaiting the assaulting columns until they arrived within 50 yards, then opening such a fire that it drove the enemy helter skelter back, the French following almost into the town. Like ourselves, they lost a number of men, but with a far greater loss to the foe. General Canrobert considers twenty thousand Russians were put *hors de combat* during the day. If so, the presence of two Grand Dukes, Constantine and Nicholas, who arrived with Osten Sacken, has merely urged their troops on to destruction. It is said that Canrobert held up his hands in astonishment on hearing that we had left so important and so exposed a position as A B totally unprotected by fortifications ; now that the horse has been stolen we are shutting the stable door, but Lord Raglan seems most apathetic on such points. We have been here now six weeks, and the Russians might easily have destroyed our stores and transports in Balaklava any time during the first month; the lines are now strong, but the thanks are due to Sir E. Lyons' strong remonstrances and Sir Colin Campbell's energy, rather than to my Lord's prevision. I suppose forty years at a desk, examining little petty details, must be a bad school for a Commander of a large army, who should look at things *en grand*.

Whether reinforcements have been asked for with proper urgency I don't know, but we certainly want them much. The siege goes on but slowly, and may last an indefinite time, whilst we are now ourselves besieged. The valley of the Chernaya is lined with Russian troops, and there is little doubt that the enemy is superior in numbers to us, which is a state of affairs that *ought* not to leave us ultimately masters. However, I have the greatest confidence in our pluck and endurance, and I suppose we shall go on through the winter as at present — gradually advancing, occasionally repulsing assaults — and that in due course of time we shall get reinforcements, lick the outside army, and get into the place. My private opinion is that Balaklava will not be attacked, the whole Russian energies must be expended in raising the siege. Balaklava is merely an outpost, and its capture, although

## ILLNESS OF CAPTAIN DACRES.

it would greatly inconvenience us, would not have any effect of that sort.

November 8th.—Weather still fine. No news from the front. The "Prince" just arrived with the 46th Regiment, and detachments for others, making two thousand men altogether.

"SANSPAREIL,"

Balaklava,

November 10th, 1854.

MY DEAR HEATH,

I am quite knocked up and unable to leave the ship. You must please to come here and look to the port duties, for I am quite unequal to it, and shall be for a day or two. I have cot slung and everything ready for you on board "Sanspareil." Bring a tooth brush, and I will not ask you to use a razor.

Yours sincerely,

S. L. DACRES.

*LETTER No. 19.*

H.M.S. "SANSPAREIL,"

Balaklava,

November 18th, 1854.

A very handsome birthday present have I just received from Admiral Dundas in the shape of a commission as acting Captain of the "Sanspareil," whose late Captain (Dacres) has invalided. Knowing he intended to go I had been privately speculating on the changes that would probably take place, and thought it possible that I might perhaps come in for the "Samson," or "Furious," or "Retribution," but that on the other hand the Admiral might consider that such an appointment would certainly not be confirmed and that it was not worth his while to offer, or anyone's to accept it, so you may guess how agreeably I was surprised at receiving so grand an appointment. I suppose there can be but little doubt as to my being confirmed to the rank, although unless ordered home I am not likely to keep the ship.

Hore is my successor in the "Niger." I am glad that so good a fellow is appointed, as I should

## WRECK OF THE "PRINCE"

not have liked my shipmates of four years and a half to get into bad hands. His vessel, the "Beagle," is given to Lieutenant Hewitt, who has very much distinguished himself in command of a Lancaster gun in the trenches; so we flatter ourselves that Admiral Dundas deserves great credit for making such good appointments, instead of merely looking out for his private friends.

I have no journal letter ready, there has been no fighting with muskets and bayonets of any consequence since I last wrote, but a most dreadful one with the winds and waves, and a sad loss both of life and property. We lost eight transports here, thirteen at Katcha, and an unknown but large number at Eupatoria. All the English men-of-war are safe, but the French have lost one line of battle ship and one steamer, and the Turks a line of battle ship. Our greatest loss is in the "Prince" steamer, which had an immense quantity of warm clothing on board for the troops, and in the transport "Resolute" with small-arm ammunition. The letter-bag is suddenly ordered to be closed.

*LETTER No. 20.*

---

H.M.S. " SANSPAREIL,"

November 23rd, 1854.

My journal is terribly behindhand, but my excuse is hard work and want of events to describe. November 5th only comes once a year, and I suspect that, after the tremendous slaughter they suffered, the Russians will let us alone for a considerable time, but minor battles or skirmishes sink into nothing when——I fell asleep and went to bed at that point of my letter, and don't remember what I was going to end the sentence with. Minor battles and skirmishes do take place occasionally, generally in the shape of small sorties from the Russians, which take place at night, and have always been easily repulsed; but on 20th November the sortie was made from our side by the Rifles against a Russian outwork which had been pushed forward to cover skirmishers, who had from its loopholes done us a good deal of damage for the last few days. Captain Tryon conducted the business to a most successful result; they drove the Russians out and have kept the place, and turned it now against the enemy; but Captain Tryon was himself killed, to the great regret of all who knew him. An attempt was, of course, made on the 22nd to retake the place, but we had much strengthened it both in works and men, and we still hold it to-day, the 23rd.

I don't think I have given you any but a very cursory account of the dreadful gale we had here on the 14th. It began at seven in the morning and between eight and ten was at its height, the ships in harbour (I was on board "Sanspareil") all drove one on the top of the other, but being moored head and stern they were all squeezed one on top of the other, side by side, and comparatively little damage was done to them. Several took the ground, and the "Sanspareil" amongst others. The principal damage was done in self-defence by the "Avon" steamer; she had slipped her cable, and not being able to steam against the gale steered for the harbour, which you know is very narrow, she had no anchor ready to let go, and consequently ran right across and on the top of a tier of vessels, smashing paddle boxes, bowsprits, etc., etc., to an incredible extent.

When the gale broke I went to the top of the cliff and was rejoiced to see the "Niger" and all the men-of-war still riding it out, but the "Retribution," on board of which was the Duke of Cambridge, had lost her rudder, and was evidently in a very dangerous position. In the course of the afternoon, when it had lulled a little, they all came safely into harbour. The "Niger" would have weathered it out in perfect safety, but for a large transport driving right into her and smashing her channels, etc., and it is extraordinary that they should have escaped foundering. On shore the poor soldiers had their tents blown down and passed a miserable day and night, several men dying from cold and exposure. The Russians, who had at that time no tents (I mean the outside army) must have fared equally ill. It was at first thought that the "Prince," one of the eight transports wrecked outside this port, contained all the warm clothing for the use of the troops, but it seems that half of it was on board another steamer, the "Jura," which we have now in here safe. A cargo of plank has arrived for hutting, and I hope they will soon begin that work, or they will be caught by the cold with nothing warmer than tents. We have had a good deal of rain lately, which is more trying than even the cold, for half the troops are always in the open air guarding the trenches.

Reinforcements are coming to us pretty quickly, we have now sent for forty more heavy guns from the fleet, and it is supposed they will finish up the business, but I don't think it likely a shot will be fired from them in less than three weeks from this. My own grand news is my acting appointment as Captain of the "Sanspareil," whose Captain has invalided. It was quite unexpected by me, although I had a sort of presentiment that I might perhaps get one of the smaller Post Captains' steamers, if one of them were appointed here. Captains Eden, Dacres, and Graham are invalided, and I have no doubt two or three of the others would like to go. I am fortunately one mail in advance of the other acting appointments, otherwise I should fear the Admiralty putting us all back in our old places, on the plea of their being too many.

Captain Dacres left this morning, and I have only to-day felt myself really Captain. The ship you know is rather a seedy specimen of a screw line of battle ship, but the third stripe on my arm looks just as pretty all the same. My purse, too, is now filling at the rate of £700 a year instead of £300, which is a consideration for a man with a family. Wife and child were doing well on the 3rd. I am to leave soon for Kamiesh Bay, where we shall keep the screws and two other liners, the remainder going to the Bosphorus. "Retribution" comes here; she has the Duke of Cambridge on board, and I have been dining there daily while the "Niger" and "Sanspareil" stewards are arranging the cabins.

23rd November, 1854.

My Dear Captain Heath,

I have nominated you "Captain of the Port," and advise you to have the Provost-Marshal ready on all occasions when you are troubled by merchant seamen or others.

You cannot be interfered with by any senior officer in your duty of Captain of the Port—and I know you will show them every deference and respect, but keep your own duty to yourself, and have "Sanspareil" always as ready to come out as you can.

Commander Powell will probably remain in Balaclava as his ship seems very bad. Send "Niger" here, with her people, for she must go off Odessa.

Yours faithfully,

J. W. D. Dundas.

*LETTER No. 21.*

H.M.S. "SANSPAREIL,"

Balaklava, November 27th, 1854,

Finished November 28th.

Our life is a very jog trot one compared to what it has been, the reason being, I believe, that we have got so accustomed to hearing of sorties—which are invariably repulsed with great comparative loss to the Russians—that we take no notice of them, although they are made every two or three nights on the French, and occasionally, but much more rarely, upon us. The loopholed work, however, which I told you had been taken by the Rifles has been a good deal attacked, but without success, and I understand we are strengthening it much, and expect to put guns into it soon, when it will become a useful addition to our batteries. We shall to-morrow have completed the landing of the forty additional naval guns, but in the present state of the roads they cannot be got to the front under three weeks. The French last night cut down one of the Inkermann bridges and partially destroyed the road, but unless great changes have been made in the Russian positions since I saw them a fortnight ago it can only occasion a temporary inconvenience to the enemy.

My own work now consists less in active personal superintendence than it did, and more in office work; half an hour never passes without a reference of some sort to me, and the tendency is to stir one's brain up as with a stick—so difficult is it at first to keep all the different matters separate in one's head; but, as in everything else, practice makes perfect. I have received from Admiral Dundas a regular appointment or commission as Harbour Master, so that I am clearly booked for this berth as long as I remain. ——— pushed pretty hard for it, and I don't understand why he did not get it; however, here I am, and he, I believe, is on his way to Constantinople. It is an advantageous post in many respects. In the first place I suppose it will give me some extra pay; in the next place it is the most active employment a Captain of a line of battle ship could have, as bombardments of Sebastopol don't come every day; lastly, it brings me more prominently forward than I could possibly be in any other position, and therefore increases my chances of advancement. These all (on looking back) seem selfish reasons, but there is besides a real pleasure in helping on the success of our arms and in being in a position of responsibility, instead of enacting a nominal blockade of Sebastopol—from whence the enemy *will* never, *can* never, unless perfectly mad, attempt to sail out.

My ship's company seem a fine set of men; the officers very good fellows, and also good as officers. The ship herself is, as is pretty well known, a real "Sanspareil," but at the opposite end of the scale from that usually implied by the name. She is, I believe, unmatched in inefficiency as a screw line of battle ship, but still she must be far better than any mere sailing ship. My personal comforts are considerably increased by the change of ships. I was very well off for a Commander before, but I have now a suite of apartments a little smaller than those in most line of battle ships, owing to the narrowness of the vessel, still with plenty of daylight and fresh air; a nice comfortable fireplace (the fire in which I am now enjoying) for cold weather, and a delightful stern walk, going all round the stern, for warm weather. From thence I can see all round the harbour, with the Robinson Crusoe notion of being "Monarch of all I survey." On the whole I am well inclined to consider myself a very lucky fellow, and Admiral Dundas a very discerning and disinterested Commander-in-Chief.

The weather has for the last fortnight been very rainy and the troops have suffered much from exposure to it. The road between this and the camp is eight or ten inches deep in mud and the difficulty of transporting the provisions is very great, but as all the country roads must be even worse, I suppose the Russians suffer still more in that respect. Our troops have begun digging deep pits sixteen feet wide and two hundred and fifty feet long, which will be roofed when completed by the Engineers; however, they can hardly be habitable in less than three weeks from this. We are rapidly receiving reinforcements, and it is thought that when sufficient have arrived to leave our besieging works well guarded we shall, when the country becomes again practicable after the rains, sally forth against the outside Russian army. Our troops have hitherto behaved with such wonderful courage that there need be no fear for the result should such an event take place, and I don't think our Generals are likely to undertake anything rash or impracticable—I should say their fault, if any, lies rather the other way.

Speaking after the event, which is very easy, there seems little doubt we have let one or two most favourable opportunities slip through our fingers; more especially delaying after the Alma instead of pushing on (leaving four thousand or five thousand to pick up the wounded). Had we gone forward on the following day all accounts of deserters concur in stating we should have caught the enemy completely disorganised.

*LETTER No. 22.*

H.M.S. "SANSPAREIL,"

Balaklava,

December 3rd, 1854.

If I were to journalise all my own daily individual proceedings you would get a regular hotchpotch. I suppose in the course of the day I get at least thirty letters or personal applications on all sorts of subjects. First, perhaps, will come a skipper of a merchant ship complaining that another ship has done him damage, and that the skipper of that other ship says, being employed by Government, Government will of *course* do the repairs (a doctrine I don't subscribe to); then a letter from head quarters, asking my opinion as to some contemplated change in the point of embarkation of sick; then a letter from some artillery officer, stating that unless I supply him with some rope he cannot get his guns to the front; then an application for help from the commissariat in landing some particular cargo, etc., etc., etc. Luckily I have got an active and zealous assistant in Powell, commanding the "Vesuvius," and he does all the work which I used to do in the piloting line, whilst I take what may be called the diplomatic department. One day is very like another. The siege works are almost at a standstill, neither side firing much. The Russians seem to be in constant dread of an assault from the French, for they continually begin a heavy fire on some portion of the French lines at night, and no one can make out what their object can be, unless it is to repel some imaginary assault.

December 2nd.—The Russians came out and retook from us an outwork which I told you in my last had just been taken by a party of the Rifles, but in a few minutes we took it back again and we still hold it. Sickness is on the increase, and this wet weather must be very trying to all up there, but more to the soldiers than the sailors, as they are sleeping out—if sleeping it can be called—twelve hours out of every twenty-four. The heavy guns are all landed, but it is perfectly impossible to move them until the roads dry up. They are now in some places a foot deep in stiff mud, and the commissariat have given up their wheel carts altogether and turned all their beasts into pack horses; the consequence is that half rations come very frequently to those poor fellows who are quartered the farthest off. Lord Raglan takes things very coolly. I have been urging the absolute necessity of using the cavalry for commissariat horses. One step only has been taken as yet to relieve the difficulty, and that is bringing a portion of the cavalry down here, which saves the carriage of hay, etc. It may be perfectly true that men will not die of starvation on half or even quarter rations, but it is equally true that good rations are a strong prevention against sickness, and that a man in good condition will do work and stand exposure whilst a half starved man would break down. It is supposed that when the new batteries have opened fire the assault will be made *coute qui coute*, and that in case of success both flanks of the Russians will be attacked and the Russians doubled up, as the military phrase is.

My domestic affairs are getting more settled, the steward having succeeded in putting things in their places. I am very comfortable with my stove, which, however, is not yet much wanted, for the weather though rainy is mild. It blows constantly and very hard. I am afraid I am rather late for the post, but I have nothing wherewith to fill the other side, even if there was time.

*LETTER No. 23.*

H.M.S. "SANSPAREIL,"

Balaklava,

December 7th, 1854.

I hope this letter will reach you in a shorter space of time than I fear my late ones have taken, for I believe they have generally remained an extra period in the post office, owing to there being no official mail cart to take them over to Karatch Bay, which is now the point of departure of the packet. You will have heard, I hope, for certain, that which is still a little uncertain, but only a little, with me —my promotion to Post rank, as being the senior Commander in command on the 17th October. Powell got a note yesterday from Sir Edmund Lyons; it enclosed a list of promotions for the 17th, having on it Kynaston and Rogers as the Commanders who were advanced. This list had been written by the Secretary, but on the back of the paper Sir Edmund had written: "The Senior Commander of the line of battleships engaged —Frere; the Senior Commander of the sloops—

Heath"; etc., etc. So I suppose there is no doubt about it, but that they are waiting to ascertain who those seniors really are, to avoid such mistakes as were made after Acre, when, after the Commissions had been delivered, it was discovered that one of the senior lieutenants so promoted had been in Malta hospital when the battle was fought.

I have nothing new for you from the camp. We are lying on our oars waiting to get our guns up. The weather has changed this morning; if it lasts the roads will soon dry, and I hope cholera, which is again bad in camp, will cease. There are, I am told, eighty deaths a day at the front. I have lost two men within the last four days on board this ship, but there are no fresh cases. I have begun an attempt at making coffee-roasting machines, sufficient for the whole army. If successful, it will be a great boon to them, for fuel is very scarce in front, and you may conceive the desparing looks which a man, who has just come in from twelve hours' exposure to heavy rain without any cover, will cast on his green berries. The commissariat have acknowledged their inability to supply the whole allowance of salt meat in front, but they get occasional supplies of live animals from Eupatoria, and as these walk up on their own legs there has not been much deficiency in the rations as yet, except for a few days. Of course, the less men get the less able are they to stand such exposure to the weather as they have lately had. An extra cargo of pack mules is expected daily, and they would put us all at ease if they would arrive.

The Russians yesterday abandoned their encampment on the Tchernaya, but we don't know which way they have gone or what is the reason of their decampment. We are sending fifteen thousand fighting Turks (Omar Pasha's men) to Eupatoria, and it may be the Russians are gone to meet them. It may be, again, that they feared an attack where they were when we got up our reinforcements; or it may be that food had become scarce. In any case our movement looks good, as it must be a threatening one to the Russians, and is the first of an offensive description we have made against the outside army. Hutting is going on I am afraid but slowly, still some progress is making. I hope when you send the wooden houses you talk of, you will send mules to carry them up. Warm clothing is coming rapidly into the harbour, but blankets are still rather short, many having gone down in the "Prince." I have just received a congratulatory note from Sir E. Lyons announcing my promotion. He says, "You shall not go home yet awhile if I can contrive to keep you here."

## *LETTER No. 24.*

H.M.S. "Sanspareil,"
Balaklava,
December 13th, 1854.

The bad weather left us a week ago. So deep, however, was the mud on the roads, and so perfectly had it been kneaded and mixed up by the enormous traffic on it that they are hardly dry even yet; and the want of transport has been increased, first by the deaths amongst the beasts from the extra work and bad weather, and then by Admiral Boxer's slackness in forwarding others on from the Bosphorus, although urgently required to do so some time ago. A portion of the men have now to walk down their seven miles and go back laden with food for their comrades. In other respects matters are going on well, reinforcements arriving fast, no accidents to the shipping, sick-list reducing, and guns and ammunition moving to the front. But fine weather or more mules are indispensable. An order has been issued to-day for the cavalry to be used as a substitute for mules, and that is a good measure and will relieve us much.

I think I told you I had a project for roasting their coffee down here. It has succeeded very well, and with three men I roast more than one-third of the daily consumption. I shall have two more machines ready in a day or two (they are merely old oil casks mounted and fitted up with a turning handle).

We don't here discuss much whether Russia has really offered to accept the four points, but we do discuss the singularly Napoleonic despatch written by Lord Raglan respecting the battle of Inkerman. No doubt you all fancy that regiments and companies and, of course, individual men, were all marshalled in their ranks, as if in Hyde Park; but all eye-witnessess to whom I have spoken say that there was the most perfect intermixture of different regiments in different divisions, and of different companies in different regiments, and even in many cases men were in their wrong companies. You saw an officer gather together a hundred men or so and rush ahead, and as to there having been any generalship displayed, or attempted to be displayed, there was nothing of the sort, except, perhaps, by Sir George Cathcart, and his manœuvre turned out to be a mistake and, as far as he himself was concerned, a fatal one. There never was a battle so entirely, so gloriously, won by English stout-heartedness and stubborn persevering courage amongst officers and men, and there never was one more irregularly fought, or which gave less room for the display of generalship And yet Lord Raglan is so far the only man rewarded.

## HEALTH OF THE TROOPS IMPROVING.

Reinforcements are rapidly arriving. Balaklava is pretty full, but mules are not forthcoming. We have a most active Engineer appointed to mend roads, etc., Major Hall, of the Madras Artillery, and a large body of Zouaves are helping him. I don't know whether we also give them money, but part of our payment is in rum, of which their officers complain we give them too large an allowance. They are macadamizing our road and have done about a mile. The health of the troops is improving; the deaths yesterday were but thirty-three, whilst they reached eighty on some days last week. The weather wonderfully mild; must make sleeping in the trenches quite a luxury. Blankets and other warm clothing are pouring in. I observe all people connected with commissariat or other supply departments put down any deficiencies to the loss of the "Prince." It must have been a most useful loss to them and have saved their characters on many occasions.

There is no naval or personal news to relate. I hear of another Captain (Carnegie) invaliding, and as Sir Edmund Lyons says I shall not go home if he can help it, I suppose when superseded here, I may be turned on to "Leander" or some other vessel. I am rather late with my letter, as usual, for work is heavy and time short, but I have nothing more to say. All well at Malta November 24th.

*LETTER No. 25.*

H.M.S. " SANSPAREIL,"

Balaklava,

Finished December 18th, 1854.

I took a holiday on the 15th and went as far as the naval brigade's camp, hoping to see Randolph, who went there for a day before returning home. I missed him by an hour, but being so far I took the opportunity of going further still, and rode to the extreme right and was lionised by Captains Lushington and Moorsom and by the A.Q.M.-General Colonel Percy Herbert. It has been the fashion to say that we have been idle for the last month, and I was most agreeably surprised to see that such was not the case, but that we have been pushing forward redoubts and entrenchments, until the communication between Sebastopol and the outside army has been entirely cut off by land and can only be kept up by means of the boats and steamers in the harbour.

We have advanced, I should say, one thousand yards since the battle of Inkerman, and that part of our position which before the battle was unguarded is now well secured. Our outside redoubt is between the head of the harbour and the site of what used to be the bridge over the river; the bridge, however, has been entirely destroyed, and the causeway which led to it is open to our fire within eight hundred yards. There was another point which pleased me much, and dissipated one cause of anxiety which I had heard many people who ought to know better express, viz., the existence within our camp of large quantities of firewood. The brushwood soon disappears, but it has now been discovered that the roots of the brushwood burn far better than what is above ground, and there are many weeks' (and perhaps months') supplies within reach.

The cavalry have begun to work for the commissariat, but English soldiers are certainly bad hands at adapting themselves to circumstances. You would hardly suppose that it takes two hundred and forty horses to carry a hundred and twenty sacks of bread (each sack weighing one hundredweight). It really is quite absurd to see the column going out two deep, a man on one horse leading another, with one bag piled on the top of the saddle so that there is every chance of its toppling over before it reaches its destination. They don't seem to think how much simpler it would be to sling two bags pannier fashion, and that the weight would even then not be more than that of a man in heavy marching order. Then as cavalry horses can be taught to dance, there can be no difficulty in teaching them to go in strings of eight or ten like mules, heads tied to tails, and then they would have one man to each string. Two hundred and fifty baggage horses arrived yesterday, and I suppose full rations will now be the order of the day again. Some divisions, and more particularly the 4th, have had only half allowance of meat for the last ten days.

December 18th.—It was reported last night that a Russian attack was to come off to-day, but I am writing at noon and we have heard no extraordinary firing and all seems quiet. The report was believed at head quarters for they sent in all haste for two regiments that had just landed. Guns go to the front but slowly, and ammunition still more so, and although this is a sunny day, and eight or ten more like it might hasten matters, we cannot in the present state of the roads calculate on having our batteries fully armed and ready to begin the second act of the drama before the 6th January. Our mail is a good deal overdue. I am more anxious than usual for it, as it ought to bring me word of my fate as to remaining in this ship or no. As yet I hardly consider myself as anything but a bird of passage, and take no interest in the ship herself or any trouble to learn all the ins and outs of her and her routine. Gordon, the Commander, seems to get on very well and I let him alone. The harbour work is getting less arduous, because more regular, and I am well off for assistants in Powell and Borlase. The former does the piloting; the latter is the judge advocate, and settles all the rows and quarrels in the harbour, which I have no time for; and I am general administrator and correspondent of all the departments on shore and afloat.

*LETTER No. 26.*

H.M.S. "SANSPAREIL,"

Balaklava,

December 22nd, 1854.

Rain has set in again, but three hundred mules have arrived; the one event about balances the other, with a small preponderance of good on the side of the mules—and having told you that, I have told you pretty nearly all there is to tell. Small sorties, always repulsed more or less successfully, are now so common that no one thinks of them or talks of them. There was one a few nights ago which created a little more excitement than usual, because we lost two officers killed, and two made prisoners; the fact being, I am told, that the picket, sentries and all, were asleep.

The French have lent a division consisting of six thousand men to take up the ground hitherto held by our extreme left, and this has allowed us to strengthen our right—the scene of Inkerman—where, from having advanced so much lately, we had extended, and therefore, as far as men are concerned, weakened our front. The late reinforcements have cheered everyone up, and one hears a good deal less croaking. The guns, as I have previously said, go to the front but slowly. This you will understand when I tell you it takes sixty horses to get them over one portion of the road. There are about fifty of the new lot of guns and mortars gone to the front, but a small portion only of the ammunition. The French help us much, they carry up our shot and bring down our sick, and they are macadamizing our road. It is said they are getting impatient, and that Canrobert, when passing through the camp, is occasionally murmured at for being slow to assault.

Admiral Dundas left yesterday, and has, I suppose, virtually given up the command. It is difficult under these circumstances to know how to address a public letter. I hit upon the following plan—whilst the two Admirals were both in Karatch Bay I used no name, but addressed to "The Commander-in-Chief;" now that they have separated, I address to "Sir Edmund Lyons," etc., etc., etc., without naming Commander-in-Chief. Rumour says that on the arrival of three or four more screw liners, which are expected, another naval attack will be made. The "Sanspareil" cannot be left out in such an event, for Sir Edmund would never pay so bad a compliment to the officers and ship's company that backed him up so well on the first occasion.

I have received my Post Captain's commission, it is dated the 13th November. The Whigs are said to be destitute of chivalrous feeling and to be cold and unromantic. This is a strong case for those who think so. Why in the world when they give promotions as rewards for a certain event don't they date them on the same day? My grandchildren will never believe that I was promoted for the bombardment of Sebastopol, because Arthur's wife will have taught them history so well that they will know that that event took place on the 17th October, whereas they will find in O'Bourne's Naval Biography that Grandpapa was made a Post Captain on the 13th November. Mary has sent me the prettiest possible picture of the boy at six weeks old; he is very like me—as much so as the difference of age will allow, I think. My last news of Mary is 7th December, all well. She wants to go to England, but until my destination is settled it is of no use attempting to fix her's. I am inclined to wish that for the baby's sake she should, having begun the winter in a warm climate, remain there until it ends, and not leave Malta under any circumstances before April.

I am puzzled to know what to expect for myself if the ship stops out; she is the most fit for this harbour, and that axiom being laid down the difficulty arises that whereas my seniors have a fair claim to this ship, I have an equally fair claim to this harbour. The mail has been in a day or two, but our letters are still at Karatch Bay, and I have not yet received anything later from England than my birthday letters of November 18th, and therefore have no congratulations from any of you. I see on a rough estimate about one-fifth of the last hundred Post Captains on the list were promoted at or under my age, which is a larger number than I should have expected.

*LETTER No. 27.*

---

H.M.S. "SANSPAREIL,"

Balaklava,

December 30th, 1854.

I suppose I ought to send another journal letter, although there is nothing of importance to record. The weather, which with you begins a conversation merely as a matter of course, is with us a matter of serious importance, and we watch it with the greatest anxiety. With the exception of Christmas Day and the next, when there was a hard frost accompanied by a fall of snow, we have had mild weather, and to-day has been like a warm day at the end of October in England. But previous rains have thoroughly soaked the soil, and the roads are still as bad as ever.

Yesterday I had an interview with the railroad engineer, he wants his main line to run along the beach road, which I object to on two grounds: first that for the safety of the large ships they must lay their anchors out across the beach road; and secondly because if any one article of provisions should not be forthcoming from the transports at the proper time, all those articles which are landed behind them would have to wait until the first article arrived and could be despatched. I propose that the next street should be selected for the main road, and that sidings from the beach wharfs should be led into it. It appears that Mr. Campbell is not engineer-in-chief, and all he can do is to make a note of the objections and await the arrival of his chief.

I have had the honour of assisting at a Council of War, called by the Generals to inquire whether the Admirals would undertake to bring Omar Pasha's army over to Eupatoria, and when there to bring their food over from the Bosphorus. They have undertaken it. I don't suppose there is any great secret in this, but it is as well not to talk of it until the newspapers lead the way. Canrobert reminds me much of the picture of Cromwell, he wears a short surtout coat, buttoned up, and a broad red woollen belt round his waist. He is short but strongly built and active looking, and I should think not much above forty-five. Mules are arriving, and the supplies now go to the front with tolerable regularity. The French help us up with our ammunition, and I suppose that in a fortnight, say the 12th of January, the new bombardment will begin. The Russian outside army has left our neighbourhood, frightened we suppose by the large arrivals of Turks at Eupatoria. It is said they are again entrenching themselves on the Alma.

From what Sir E. Lyons said yesterday I don't expect to get away under a fortnight. I believe Drummond is my successor, and he has to hunt his ship round the Coast of Circassia. I remain until his arrival. My feelings as to going home or not are of a very mixed nature. I should like to go in and out of Sebastopol Harbour in my ship, and on the other hand I should like to set up Mary's home and leave her (if I should leave her in the spring which I hardly think probable) snugly settled in her own house. I hope to get permission to take her with me from Malta, which will be very pleasant, to say nothing of being very economical. The "Crimean Army Ships" with good things to be sold at cost price are daily expected. Never was a greater mistake made, there are at least twenty private traders now in the harbour, and if their profits are destroyed we must trust to the Crimean Army Fund being made a perpetual thing. Free trade principles are evidently not in vogue at the Royal Yacht Club.

## LETTER No. 28.

H.M.S. "SANSPAREIL,"

Balaklava,

January 9th, 1855.

As you will see by the date I am still here. I don't know when I shall start, I wait for Admiral Boxer who relieves me. Sir Edmund Lyons seems to think I shall be here another fortnight, as Admiral Stopford left the Bosphorus for Malta on the 28th December, whence he will return to take Admiral Boxer's place in the Bosphorus, and the latter will not start for this until relieved. The "Tribune" has, however, returned from Circassia, and if I were Sir Edmund I should certainly think it a serious business to detain "Sanspareil," as a time contract has been made for putting new engines into her, and every day's delay here reduces by so much the chance of her being ready for the spring campaign. We have had four days of very cold weather, thermometer 17 degrees at night, but I don't hear of many losses in consequence. Two or three officers have died *asphyxiés* from charcoal in their tents. A warning general order has in consequence been issued on the subject. For the last few days large parties have been employed carrying up provisions on their backs to make a depôt in front, in case of the roads becoming quite impassable, and the frost has been favourable for this work. One sees plenty of theodolites and measuring chains walking about the country, but no material or navvies have yet arrived. I cannot conceive that the railroad can be made under three weeks from the date of beginning it, and as no one yet knows even whether there is water for feeding the engines on the hill, I should put down six weeks as a very moderate allowance of time for completing the whole concern. I don't wish to discourage the thing but should like to see a thousand mules arrive in the meantime. The beach is covered with huts; they are not likely, however, to get to the front, except in very limited numbers, for it will take two hundred men to carry one. Three have been set up close to the town and look very comfortable.

The siege is quite at a standstill; a few shot fired on both sides daily but nothing more. Eight hundred French come down daily and carry up two hundred shells for us, and so preparations for the second act of the drama are going slowly on—but only slowly. We flatter ourselves, in spite of what "Our Own Correspondents" say, that the harbour is in very fair order. I have a first-rate

## THE SHIPS AND THE HARBOUR. 139

working assistant in Powell, and certainly if any one thing connected with the expedition is carefully attended to and looked after it is the anchoring of the ships. "Our Correspondent" may be a better judge of whether it is well or ill done than we are; but we are quite contented and our consciences quite clear, and I am told the merchant skippers who are used to Liverpool docks, etc., quite bear us out in our good opinion of our doings.

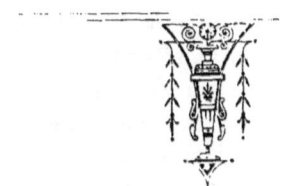

## LETTER No. 29.

H.M.S. "SANSPAREIL,"

Balaklava,

January 12th, 1855.

Still no signs of Admiral Boxer, and therefore no preparations for the homeward-bound voyage. I read last night in the *Evening Mail*, of December 15th to 18th, "Our Own Correspondent" on Balaklava Harbour, and am perfectly astonished that a man can sit down and write such downright untruths. I can understand that one whose profession is that of "Graphic Describer" will be constantly prone to exaggerate a little for the sake of points and effect; but he has gone a long way beyond that. It is quite possible that mine may not be the best system of mooring ships, but he says there is no system at all, whereas there is a very strict one, and I am sure I speak within bounds when I say that not one vessel in thirty comes in without our assistance as pilots. I have done unwisely, perhaps—it depends on the result, which I don't know—but I have in my civil capacity as Harbour Master sent round a circular to the Masters of Transports asking their opinion as to the justice of *The Times*' statements.* I don't intend publishing it, even if the answers are favourable, or going to war with *The Times*, but I shall perhaps be cross-questioned at the Admiralty, and the document would then come in very well.

I see there is a great deal of talk about the "Prince," and I know that all the authorities have been called on to make reports. I put the chief blame on the Master's shoulders. He could not have been a good seaman to have lost his two first anchors when bringing up, and to have remained at anchor with his third was bad enough; but to cut the masts of a screw ship away after slipping instead of before is a clear proof of incompetency. The "Melbourne" once lost her topmasts by accident and her screw was jammed for forty-eight hours.

Ammunition still goes to the front, and a store of biscuit is being forwarded as a reserve. Horses are more abundant than of yore, but they are animals which arrive half starved from Varna, and as they are not looked after and have no shelter here their life is but a short one. A cargo of Alicant mules is expected, and I have undertaken to build a shed to hold them on condition that regular grooms shall be appointed to feed and look after them when their day's work is over. I began

* Vide Page 142.

at it yesterday, and hope to have it up before the mules arrive, and that this may be the beginning of a better system with the commissariat animals. The harbour is full of huts, but there is not much chance of getting them up in any numbers to the front. Some have been set up in the immediate neighbourhood of the port and give great satisfaction.

The naval brigade is being reduced by taking away the crews of ships ordered to England. I suppose this is merely an act of justice to the men and has nothing to do with the prospects of the siege. The weather is again cold, thermometer about 28 deg. I hear sickness has rather decreased. We embark about twelve hundred a week for Scutari.

### BALAKLAVA HARBOUR.

Copy of a paragraph in *The Times:* —

"Will it be credited that with all our naval officers in Balaklava with nothing else to do—with our *embarras de richesses* of Captains, Commanders, and Lieutenants—there is no more care taken for the vessels in Balaklava than if they were colliers in a gale off Newcastle? Ships come in and anchor where they like, do what they like, go out when they like, and are permitted to perform whatever vagaries they like, in accordance with the old rule of 'higgledy piggledy, rough and tumble,' combined with 'happy go lucky.'"

ENTRANCE TO BALAKLAVA HARBOUR.

BALAKLAVA HARBOUR.

Described by the "Times" Correspondent as "Higgledy Piggledy," "Rough and Tumble."

Circular to Captains of Transports.

H.M.S. "Sanspareil,"

Balaklava,

January 10th, 1855.

Gentlemen,

My attention has been called to the annexed paragraph in *The Times* newspaper. I am about to return to England, and should be glad to know whether, in your opinions, the strictures in that paragraph are just or unjust.

The question is not whether ships should be moored up and down or athwartships—on this plan or on that plan; but it is whether there is at present any system at all—whether the ships are placed in any regular order, or whether (as the "Correspondent" states) they are left to anchor where and when they please. I should be glad also to know whether you consider that your interests and welfare in those points specially belonging to a harbour master's duties are attended to or neglected by us—whether, in fact, there is any foundation whatever for the statements that "there is no more care taken of you than if you were colliers in a gale off Newcastle."

Your obedient servant,

L. G. Heath,

Harbour Master.

### Answers.

"The pilotage of the port under Captain Powell, requiring the largest ships to be handled under critical circumstances, has caused me repeatedly to express my most unqualified admiration. This duty has called for incessant labour, and it has been bestowed with the most untiring zeal and with an ability not to be surpassed by the most practised hand. I consider the present state of the harbour a marvel of exact arrangement."

"I beg permission to express my opinion that the harbour arrangements, with the prompt assistance given to all vessels, are perfect."

"We concur in saying it is false to say that ships take up their position in this harbour as they please; and taking into consideration the smallness and inconvenience of the harbour, we think the ships are moored in the most efficient manner, both as regards safety and expedition."

"As you are now on the eve of your departure for England, I cannot permit you to leave without acknowledging my grateful sense of the courtesy and gentlemanly consideration I have experienced from yourself as harbour master, as also from your most able assistant, Commander Powell, to whom I am much indebted for the science displayed in the management of my ship whilst piloting her into and out of this very snug but tortuous harbour, when the most profound judgment is required. Indeed, the zeal and ability exhibited by you both, early and late, together with your arrangements and general good management, have excited the admiration of my nautical friends."

---

There are thirteen documents much in the same style signed by forty-seven individuals, including the Masters of all the large steamers.

---

REPORT ON THE WRECK OF THE TRANSPORT "PRINCE."

H.M.S. "SANSPAREIL,"
Balaklava,
January 2nd, 1855.

MY DEAR SIR EDMUND LYONS,

I have carefully thought over the subject mentioned in the despatches which you gave me to read, and have come to the conclusion that the principal cause of the loss of the "Prince" was the incompetency of her Master.

The best of seamen bringing a long unwieldy ship, like the "Prince," to an anchor may be obliged if under sail to do so with fresh way on to avoid contact with other ships, but under steam there can be no possible excuse for doing so, and therefore no possible excuse for losing an anchor and cable, even if the latter were not clinched, still less for losing two.

Again, no person, with any knowledge of the peculiar danger there is of fouling a screw, would have cut away his masts *after* getting under weigh. If it should be necessary to get rid of them he should do so before slipping and not after. The well-known history of the "Melbourne," whose screw was jammed for two days by the accidental carrying away of her topmasts should have taught him better.

In the middle of November the defences of Balaklava were not anything like so strong either in entrenchments or men as they are now, and I know Captain Dacres felt with great anxiety that there was a double responsibility upon his shoulders. He felt that if the enemy should make a successful attack it would be of the utmost importance that as few ships as possible should be in the harbour, in order that those which were there should have a chance of escape and not hinder one another. On the other hand he knew the season was advancing, and that although no warning had yet been given (not a single vessel having as yet been driven on shore or received any damage), still an anchorage in forty or forty-five fathoms on an open coast could not but be dangerous.

I have personally had more experience in bringing ships into Balaclava Harbour than any one else, and I would certainly not undertake to bring such a vessel as the "Prince" safely in with a strong southerly wind. "Of two evils choose the least" is a good maxim. The danger of bringing the vessel in was known; the tremendous gale that awaited her was unknown. It is easy to reason after events, and one is apt to forget that if the "Prince" had been wrecked coming in, and the gale of the 14th had not occurred to justify the attempt, there would have been the same outcry on the subject as there is now.

I do not know whether Captain Christie was aware of the "Prince" having but one anchor left. There can be no doubt that he ought to have been aware of it, and that in that case he ought not to have allowed her to remain at anchor. On this point the whole blame rests with him, because as Principal Agent of Transports he controlled their movements; but I think that under the circumstances the Captain of the "Prince" should not have come into the roadstead without orders, nor with orders without remonstrating.

I am, therefore, once more led to conclude that the incompetency of the Captain was the principal cause of the disaster.

Yours very truly,

L. G. HEATH.

*LETTER No. 30.*

H.M.S. "SANSPAREIL,"

Balaklava,

January 19th, 1855.

How you must all be wondering and puzzling what the appointment is which I expect. Whatever it may be, it has been offered in such handsome terms that I could not help accepting, however tempting prospects of Moorhurst may be. Now I may as well tell you; don't you think so? I don't know how much a year it is, nor any details of that sort. I have been very busy lately building a shed to hold two hundred and fifty mules expected from Alicant. I anticipate it will be the only thing that is not "too late," as Lord Grey said. — Then perhaps the appointment is " Carpenter to the Forces " ?

A man has this moment left me who came to get help in making sledges; he was sent down expressly to superintend them, but the frost left us last night, and a boat would be a better conveyance to the camp now than a sledge ; sledges are clearly " too late " for this frost—however, they may come in again. The cold has been very severe, and many men have been frost-bitten and lost their toes. Thermometer all one day at 22 deg., and down one night to 17 deg. Fahrenheit.

Large working parties from different regiments are erecting stores for the Commissariat and additional huts for hospitals, and altogether there is a good deal of energy at work. Want of mules, railroad or transport of some description is the *great* want, almost the only one. The system of having the beasts under the Commissariat is a bad one, and I hope to persuade Lord Raglan to begin a new and better system with the two hundred and fifty expected mules.—" Then it must be Stable Keeper?"

*LETTER 31.*

H.M.S. "SANSPAREIL."

Balaklava,

January 23rd, 1855.

I suppose a letter with nothing in it is still better than none at all. I am expecting Admiral Boxer in about two days, and I shall then be off to Malta as fast as the "Sanspareil's" ricketty engines will take me. There I am to have ten days' leave of absence, after which, if the Admiralty approves of Sir Edmund Lyons's suggestions, I shall be turned back eastward, and Mary will trudge on to England. I shall leave with the satisfaction of having been the cause of a great improvement in what is now in the greatest disorder of any department connected with the army. I told you I was building stabling for mules; I have now succeeded in getting a cavalry officer and dismounted cavalry soldiers to attend to the grooming, feeding, and stabling department, and by a letter I received yesterday from Lord Raglan I find the example is going to be followed up, and stabling is to be built immediately for some buffaloes that are expected.

## MULES IN GREAT REQUEST.

Sick still pour down upon Balaklava; eight hundred a week are sent away to Scutari, etc. The weather is again mild, but the melting of eighteen inches of snow has made the plain deeper in mud than ever. Some of my mules are to be lent to carry up huts, which they will do at the rate of seven or eight a day; there seems no other chance of getting them up in any numbers. The loan of these animals has been wrung out of Mr. Filder with great difficulty, and it would seem that under the present system you must send out horses as well as fireplaces with each hut.

*LETTER No. 32.*

---

H.M.S. " SANSPAREIL,"

Khersonese,

February 3rd, 1855.

Here I am at last fairly clear of Balaklava and fairly started, if not on my homeward voyage, at all events on one of relaxation and pleasure. I think I am leaving just in time, for although I feel in as good health as I ever did in my life there is yet something wrong, for a chip of my knuckle which should have healed in four or five days has been now five weeks unhealed, and not only that but has spread into a nasty looking wound ; and the same thing has happened to the knuckle of one of my toes, on the top of which a boot had rubbed a hole. Change of air is the grand remedy in such cases, and although I only arrived here yesterday I fancy there is an improvement already.

I don't think I have written to you for ten days or so. The events during that time have not been very grand or exciting, but on the whole I think matters are improving. I have told you all about *my* mules, as I have got to call them ; they are comfortably housed, and their stabling and grooming, feeding, etc., is under a cavalry officer with a staff of sergeants, etc. This is not only a good move in itself, but it has produced fruit in causing the same accommodation to be provided beforehand for a hundred and eight big buffaloes just arrived. The railroad ships have begun to come, and the first batch of navvies had cleared the ground for their house before I came away yesterday. They expect in three weeks to have a single line of rails laid as far as the crest of the great plateau on which the army is encamped.

Three days ago I took leave of Lord Raglan. Being so far on the road I went on to the French entrenchments, and it may be interesting to you to know that I rode a horse called St. Arnaud, a present from the late French Commander-in-chief to Lord Raglan. The French have seven and a half miles of zigzags and parallels, the principal portion of them forming two sets of approaches of this description. I suppose you know the general principle as well as I do—it is that when one parallel is made (which serves as cover for the besieging troops) advancing zigzags are made towards the front, but zigzaged at such angles that people behind them are still under cover. After advancing by these means a certain distance, another parallel is formed for the same purpose as the first, and then another advance, and so on. I went up to their furthest, or third parallel, which is only a hundred and ten yards from the front of the Russian flag staff battery. The top of the parapet is formed of bags filled with earth, and at intervals small holes are left for the double purpose of spying and shooting with rifles at the enemy. The first curious thing I saw, and one which was a good example of the sort of life soldiers in such circumstances are accustomed to, was a party of Frenchmen, under an officer, who were employed in improving the trenches. They were standing looking at a broken iron water pipe which ran (when unbroken) through their ground, and they told me they had just been saved the hard work of destroying it themselves by a lucky cannon shot, which had fallen on it and broken it for them without touching one of their party. It was very curious to look at the enemy's guns within almost a stone's throw of them, but I confess the peculiar twang of Minie rifle balls passing, as far as one could guess, within a foot of one's head was—although very exciting—not very pleasant. The Russians posted for this express purpose are excellent marksmen, and as they probably fired on seeing the tip of one's cap, or something moving, the chances are that the balls did not really pass much more than a foot from one.

## THE FRENCH MINES.

There are two mines made by the French; one is completed, and reaches beneath the Russian works; the other, into which I went, has twenty yards further to go. It is a passage about four feet square, the ventilation is kept up by means of a rotatory fan at the mouth. The men working at the further end sit down and dig out with crow bars; others, also sitting down, shovel what is thus removed into four-wheeled trucks, which are driven along on a wooden railway to the mouth, whence the stuff is drawn up in buckets. It was very hot up at the further end, and I should think on a frosty night there would be plenty of volunteers for the work. I think I have somewhere read of mines and counter mines having met, and I could imagine the desperation of such a combat with crowbars as would then take place. I am glad to have been within twenty yards of Sebastopol. This third parallel, being the nearest to the Russian works, is of course the one most the object of attack by the Russian sorties, and many sanguinary fights have there taken place. In one of them the Russians succeeded in carrying off three small mortars, which had been used with very small charges to throw shells just the one hundred and eight yards over the Russian parapets.

Catching a Russian is I see almost like snaring a hare, for the French have all along the inner side of this parallel, at about three feet down from the top, driven short stakes at intervals of three or four yards, between these stakes they have stretched an iron wire, and it is hoped that when next the Russians succeed in clearing the top of the parapet their feet will catch in the wire, and they will tumble head foremost on the bayonets of the defenders. This device has only quite recently been adopted, and no assault has since been made to test its utility.

I should think there were fifteen hundred men guarding the third parallel, all looking jolly enough. The mail had just arrived, and the officers in groups were discussing *La Presse* or the *Moniteur*, and asked us with some eagerness what we thought of the prospects of peace. I wanted to gather their sentiments on the subject, but came to no conclusion; the most common feeling seemed one rather of indifference. Just what one might expect from people with a knowledge of the hardships of such a campaign and a distant glimmering of a speedy return to the comforts of *La Belle France* on one side, and on the other with a soldier's anxiety to take by force of arms the proud fortress that had so long and so successfully resisted them.

This expedition to the French lines took up the whole day, and no time was left for going over to the English, and taking a last look at the few acquaintances and people in whom I am interested amongst them. Richard Crofton has a brother here in the Engineers; I have not seen him since he landed, but I then had the satisfaction of supplying him with a frame work and canvas bedstead, to keep him off the wet ground. Fitzroy, now Captain Fitzroy, I saw a fortnight ago, looking very well. A few Malta acquaintances I should like to have seen, to report their appearance to their wives on my arrival at Malta.

Admiral Boxer arrived on the 31st, and from the short talk I had with him I am afraid instead of "putting things to rights," which he conceives is his mission, he will make a very pretty hotchpotch. He says his orders are "to command at Balaklava," and his idea of doing that seems to be an interference at once (without waiting for gaining local experience of any sort) with every department, whether naval or military, which he finds established in the neighbourhood. As his plan and mine are the direct opposites of one another, one of us must be very wrong. I joined the Admiral here on the evening of the 1st. He takes a hundred men from this ship to man the "Royal Albert," which came out only partially manned. Discharging these men, taking in old stores, invalids, etc., will detain me until this afternoon, and then, wind and weather permitting, I am off for the Bosphorus and Malta. There I expect to be stopped by electric telegraph, and after ten days' leave of absence to return—I suppose I may now let out my secret to the family, but *to the family only*—" Principal Agent of Transports, *vice* Christie superseded." The Admiral this evening showed me his letter on the subject to the Admiralty. I am too modest to repeat his eulogies of myself, but they were so strong that I think the appointment next thing to certain. His praises of Christie in all respects but fitness for this particular work were equally strong, and if the latter is dismissed his fall will, I am very glad to say, be as gentle a one as possible. The post is a very important one and a good deal beyond my standing. I look on it as not much below that of a Junior Flag Officer. I have some doubt whether my business habits are equal to the duties, but the responsibility of selecting has been the Admiral's, and I can only do my best.

PRIVATE AND CONFIDENTIAL.

H.M.S. "AGAMEMNON,"

January 14th, 1855.

MY DEAR HEATH,

I may tell you in strict confidence that I have to propose to the Admiralty a successor to Christie. It is at this juncture a post of the highest importance, and whoever may be appointed by the Admiralty may consider it a signal proof of the confidence of the Board. Now I know no man so fit for it as you are. Shall I propose you?

A more honourable and responsible appointment could not be given to you, in which your sea-time would be going on, and you would be establishing a claim to almost any appointment within the gift of the Board. Captain Christie is borne as supernumerary in the "Fisgard," in order that his time may count.

I send this and two accompanying notes through headquarters, and the dragoon will wait for your answers to the other two. This, you may possibly (though I hope not) wish to have a night to reflect upon, but in any case let me have your answer to this to-morrow.

Yours,<br>E. Lyons.

H.M.S. "Agamemnon,"

January 15th, 1855.

My Dear Heath,

I hear that the roads may be impassable, so I send the "Arrow" round for your answer to my proposal of yesterday, and I do hope it may be an affirmative one. My letter to the Admiralty must go at 7 a.m. to-morrow, so I shall like to have your answer as soon as may be. If you say "Yes," I will write to the Admiralty to stop you at Malta by telegraph *via* Marseilles. Take into consideration that you will be really rendering your country *great* service at a critical moment of need. You need have no delicacy about Christie, for if you are not appointed some one else will be.

E. L.

H.M.S. "SANSPAREIL,"
Balaklava,
January 14th, 1855.

MY DEAR SIR EDMUND LYONS,

I cannot tell you how flattered I felt on receiving your offer this afternoon, but I am glad you gave me a few hours for consideration, as I might otherwise have thought I had been led by those feelings without having allowed reason to step in for her share in the discussion. The more I think of it the more I see that however doubtful I may be of doing much better than my predecessor, however much I may hesitate about going out of the regular working line of the service, and however much I may regret the putting off of domestic arrangements, still the appointment is so far beyond my standing, so far more important than any I could hope to hold, that I cannot help seeing that I should be mad not to accept your offer.

I now do so with much gratitude, and much pride at having been selected by you.

Yours very sincerely,
L. G. HEATH.

*LETTER No. 33.*

Written apparently in February, 1855.

L.G.H.

I think I may as well wind up this series of journal letters by a sort of review of the campaign, premising that the opinions I shall advance are given and were formed, most of them, after the events which I criticise took place. This would not be fair if I were a rival General, or at all professed to have been able at the time to manage matters better than they were managed; but as a looker-on, and a writer in a small way of history, it is, I think, quite legitimate.

Prince Napoleon, the General of Division, now gone home, is said to have described the campaign in these terms—" The conception of an attack on Nicholas's stronghold was 'une audace,' the landing was 'une audace,' the battle of Alma was 'une audace,' and so was the march on Balaklava, and the sitting down on the heights south of Sebastopol; but there it stopped, and the one 'audace' which might have gloriously finished the campaign was wanting." I agree with him to a great extent, but I think the great original mistake was fighting the battle of Alma in the afternoon instead of the forenoon. We were the aggressors, and could choose our own time; we had a skirmish the previous evening and knew the enemy was in force, and I think we chose our position for encamping that night too far off. I don't know if there is any fixed military maxim on the subject, but it seems clear to me that it is the interest of the aggressor to have as much of the day before him as possible, to improve his victory if he gains it; and that of the attacked to put off his opponent, and delay him as much as possible, for the opposite reason.

What were the results of the Alma? What might they have been if the victorious troops had marched on but five or six miles in pursuit? What we did was to gain a great victory, and take what was then one of the outposts of Sebastopol; and in doing so we gained more than the actual victory in the prestige which was attached to it. This advantage which we gained is, I consider, the measure of what we lost by not following up our advantage. All reports agree in stating that on reaching their baggage the Russian army was in perfect confusion, and that the whole of their artillery was left for two days unguarded on the banks of the next river, the Katcha. A few hours' pursuit would have turned the Russian retreat into a Russian rout. But even if we were obliged to halt that night on the field of battle, would Napoleon or Wellington have remained (I forget how many days) for the sake of the wounded? Would not either of them have pushed on with the main body of the army, leaving a division of soldiers and a division of the fleet to look after the sufferers? Advancing leisurely as we did the road was found strewed with *débris* of all sorts, showing plainly what would have happened with more energy on our side.

Many people here, and I believe Sir Edmund Lyons amongst them, blame the march round to the south. I am quite of the contrary opinion and think *that* the saving point for the military reputation of the Allied Generals. That march having been successful, it seems *now* clear that an immediate attack on the town would also have been successful, and that it might have been foreseen that all subsequent making and arming of earthworks by ourselves, drawing our material from a port seven miles distant, must be overmatched by similar works with guns drawn from the immediate neighbourhood. I think an opinion I once heard set forth that Sir John Burgoyne considered himself a lecturer on practical siege making for the benefit of the young Engineers, with a real Sebastopol for his black board and an allied army for his chalk and long stick, is not far from the true statement of the the case. He is said to be seventy-four, and therefore naturally wedded to old opinions and old prescriptive routine, and he has, without doubt, great influence with Lord Raglan. Sir Edmund Lyons says Sir John's sole reason for objecting to an immediate attack was the existence of a wretched round tower with four guns on its top ; but yet he allowed earthworks to grow up night and day, not only round that tower, in rows two and three deep, but also round what was then an almost entirely open and defenceless town, without the slightest attempt at annoying the workmen—saying only that "all he saw could be knocked down in twenty-four hours." He said this to me on the beach at Balaklava, and a swell French officer standing by his side added "un coup de pied suffit." I do not think we fired a single shot from the 26th September until our batteries opened on the 17th October. I forgot to mention that the round tower is not a round tower at all, it is round towards Balaklava, but only a semi-circle, and is or rather was open in the rear. What a reward this discovery would have been to one more "audace!"

The bombardment began on the 17th October, the fleets were to take part in it, and it had been arranged that the French starting from Kamiesh should form in succession in a line for the attack of the forts on the south side, and that the English, commencing from what we call the Wasp Battery, should form in succession round Constantine and attack the northern defences. This plan seemed to me good, but at the last moment Admiral Hamelin persuaded Admiral Dundas not to come down from the northward, but to consider himself part of the French fleet and to form in succession on the leading French ship. The only reason I can conceive for this change was that Hamelin thought there would probably be a gap between the two fleets if the original plan were carried out, and that his leading ship would be singled out for a sort of cross fire from both sides of the harbour. The French plan was adopted, with the exception of the "Albion," "Arethusa," "Agamemnon," "London," and "Sanspareil," the three last of which are the only ships that did any real good, for all the French and all the English that followed the French were either much too far off or much too late in action. Some ships were not half an hour in action. I don't think that, however conducted, the naval attack could have been very successful, except as a powerful diversion; but the distance at which the French ships and the English which formed on them were brought into action will be a fair subject of criticism for the historian of the Crimean campaign.

The battle of Inkerman would probably not have been fought if our right had been properly secured, and the reason that it was not properly secured was that we had undertaken a larger portion of the offensive line than our small force could fairly cover. What the real reason of this was I cannot say, but suppose it must have been either ignorance as to what could be done with a given number of troops, or too much good nature and *bonhommie* in Lord Raglan. I do not think, with others, that he should have insisted on keeping his original station—viz., the left of the line—because as we took and kept Balaklava as the base of our operations, I think the right of the position naturally fell to us.

Our sanitary measures have from the first been neglected. The Russians were in no position to attack us when we first came round, we had no trenches to guard, our commissariat horses were still alive, the roads were still good, and yet not a tent did we send to the front for at least ten days, and much sickness was the consequence. No roads were made, no attempt to store provisions in front, no piles of firewood collected, no regimental cook houses established; each man did for himself, and three or four times the necessary fuel was used. Houses were pulled down, which now would have been invaluable as hospitals or storehouses; not a single precautionary measure was taken with a view to a possible failure in *immediately* occupying Sebastopol. Lord Raglan is said to have had permission to order all the Mediterranean garrisons to his support: none were sent for until a fortnight after the necessity for them had become a public topic of conversation. I believe Sidney Herbert was quite right in saying that Lord Raglan's demands had always been forestalled by the supplies from England.

## MR. FILDER'S WANT OF FORESIGHT. 167

Now for Mr. Filder. His great fault has been want of foresight, and bad calculation as to the number of horses required; to which may be added a total want of even an attempt at taking care of the animals he did provide. When the roads became so bad that carts had to be given up, he allowed his bullocks to be killed and eaten; when the roads had again hardened not a dozen bullocks were forthcoming. A cargo of horses arriving to-day and numbering three hundred would be sure to be reduced to one hundred and fifty in ten days time. When the poor beasts had travelled six or seven miles, heavily laden, on wretched roads, and returned the same distance, they were turned out into an open yard, eighteen inches deep in mud, off which mud they eat their barley and chopped straw. There were no stable keepers separate from the drivers, and the latter, being as tired after their day's work as the beasts themselves, acted upon a principle which a campaigning life tends much to foster, that of looking after No. 1 first.

Regimental management must have had much to do with our misfortunes, how else can one account for regiments like the —— going bodily to hospital or the grave, whilst others, like the 57th, have not a larger proportional sick list than the "Sanspareil." But *want of roads and want of mules* have been by far our greatest enemies.

## LETTER No. 34.

Malta,

February 27th, 1855.

I arrived here on the 23rd, after a long passage of fourteen days from Constantinople, steaming almost the whole way against light westerly winds, but detained at anchor four days out of the fourteen by a strong foul wind. The "Malacca," a new experimental corvette, took the same time for her journey, and so the "Sanspareil" must not be complained of too much. On arrival here I found a notification of my commission having been sent to Sir Edmund Lyons, and I found on an interview with the hospital doctor (to whom I went as the highest authority) that he thought it would require six weeks to set up my health again. However, I feel sure he overrates my illness, and underrates the benefit of change of scene, change of occupation, and change of air. I expect to be on my return in about a fortnight from the date of my arrival, that will be on about the 10th March.

I don't know whether I told you Sir Edmund had agreed to a suggestion from me that I should live on board a small steam man-of-war, instead of shifting about from transport to transport, as Christie had done in a rather undignified manner. The "Triton" is here under repair and will suit me very well; but address all my letters, "Captain Heath, R.N., Principal Agent of Transports, Balaklava." Your intimation of the amount of my pay rather pulls down my notion of the dignity of my office, for the one may be supposed a measure of the other. I presume it was settled before the business assumed its present gigantic dimensions.

You ask for a history of the coffee-roasting. I cannot remember exact dates, but somewhere in the end of November or beginning of December I directed an experimental roasting machine to be made by the "Sanspareil" engineers out of empty oil barrels, and this was worked by "Sanspareil" men, burning wood as their fuel, and it roasted in one day sufficient for one-third of the army. I then made two more machines, and turned the three over to the army to work for themselves. They burnt charcoal instead of wood, which of itself was one reason for its roasting more slowly. But besides that, soldiers don't work like sailors, and I seldom found on my visits to the roasting-shed that the whole three machines were at work; then the charcoal made the men ill, and alterations had to be made in the building. In the meantime the "Sanspareil's" engineers had undertaken the reventing of the guns in the batteries, and not liking to break them off from there until they had finished, it was some time before more machines were made; but a fortnight before I came away there were six machines made and at work, which did the whole allowance. During the last fortnight, also, a commissariat vessel brought in roasted coffee, and therefore, if from any circumstances there should not have been enough roasted by the machines on any day, the deficiency could be made up from this cargo. There must have been one-third of the coffee roasted during the month of December and more than a half during January, and there is no excuse whatever for the whole allowance henceforward not being issued roasted.

You ask about the numbers of the British army. I send you an official document which will tell you all about them. I think it is dated 26th January, and there were at that date nearly three thousand men on board ships at Balaklava, waiting for fine weather to disembark, who are exclusive of the return. The marines, about fourteen hundred, and seamen, about nine hundred, are also to be added. I can tell you nothing about the French camp, except that as far as I could judge from my ride through a portion of it when I visited their lines, they did not seem to have so many houses or huts as we have. I shall not be surprised if this Commission, which I see is to investigate the past state of affairs out here, comes to the conclusion that the main point, in which the French differ from us, is in having an organised land transport service, such as we are now beginning to form. I *put all*, or *almost all*, our misfortunes down to the *utter* neglect of our horses and mules. The deficient supply of fodder for any larger number than that which we have had would have made us just as badly off if we had had ever so many, but that could of course have been remedied.

Mary returns to England by the first good opportunity after I leave. Her sister goes with her. All your brotherly and sisterly and motherly invitations have been discussed by us very fully, and we have come to the determination that Eastbury is her proper place, but that she is to spend such lengthy periods with you in turn as shall suffice for her to know you all thoroughly, and you her, and for her to become a regular Heath.

*LETTER No. 35.*

Balaklava,

In great haste,

March 12th, 1855.

I have only this morning read Stafford's telling and eloquent speech, as reported in the *Herald*. It confirms my opinion of his having been kind to the sick, perhaps from real kindliness of heart, but of his having taken the journey to get up political capital in the shape of grievances. The case in which he refers to me—viz., the "Candia" having arrived in Balaklava with medical comforts on board and having been told to carry them to Sulina, etc., etc.—is a regular bit of humbug. He represents it as an instance of mismanagement. The fact of the things being there is true, and of Captain Field having offered to give them up to any officer with a commission is true. He did so in a letter to me. I wrote to the principal medical officer, and was told that they had held a board on board the ship and had decided that the particular things in question were more wanted at Scutari than at Balaklava, and that they were therefore to be sent back. Could anything else have been done, and would not the Balaklava folks have been to blame if they had done otherwise? Don't believe even half what you hear from "Eye-witnesses" if Members of Parliament.

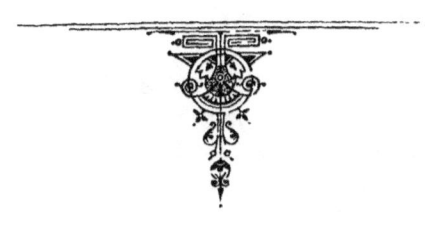

*LETTER No. 36.*

Balaklava,

March 30th, 1855.

I see your letter cost you 8d.—I suppose on account of the direction to me as Agent of Transports. Nevertheless be so good as to continue the same extravagant address, because I get the letters a day or two sooner than I should if they were addressed to H.M.S. "Triton." The said "Triton" has not yet arrived, and in the meantime I am living on board the "City of London." I suppose I must, on account of Stafford's kindly acts towards myself, relax in my hatred of his political profligacy.

As you say, this letter is not likely to reach you in time to influence your proceedings, but I am quite content that the line to be adopted should depend on your judgment, and it is a great satisfaction to me to know that you are on the *qui vive* looking out for me. I should say that as long as I am not attacked I should not move at all. There is no doubt, as you say, a wonderful jumble of dates, and a still more wonderful jumble of names and duties. Many of the things, for which if they did occur I should have been blamed, Christie is attacked for—the dead bullocks, the floating wood and hay, for instance, were all in my department, but by special arrangement with Christie his hospital ships were to look out for the first-named. I don't plead guilty to any of these things, but perhaps the dead bullocks should have been towed out of the harbour more frequently than they were; but, as I say, Christie had specifically taken over that work. The floating hay was collected as long as there was any fit for collecting. The suggestion was made to Lord Raglan that the wood should be collected for the use of the army. The answer was—" Much obliged, but we have no means of carrying it to the front." Nevertheless all the time I was there I had an enormous pile, from which any soldier who liked was at liberty to help himself (provided he did not live in Balaklava) and from whence many gun platforms were sawed by the sappers and miners.

The berthing of the ships was, *I* believe, as perfect as possible. I was responsible for the system, and Powell (whom, however, I had at first to teach and instruct to a certain extent) was responsible to me for carrying it out. I believe the best evidence that the harbour was not quite the chaos of "Our Own Correspondent"—that at all events some attempt was made at regularity—will be found in the official document headed, I think,

"Information respecting Balaklava Harbour," which I drew up for Admiral Boxer's information, and which was forwarded by Sir Edmund Lyons to the Admiralty.* It is an official document, and drawn up without any other idea than that of giving my successor all the information in my power. Mary has the circular I sent round to the Merchant Captains about *The Times* criticisms and the answers I received.† I write by this mail to tell her to send them to you at once. I observed in Galignani's report of (I think) Mr. Clay's evidence that "the Harbour Masters were active," etc., which *The Times* of course leaves out.

---

\* Vide Next Page.   † Vide Page 143.

H.M.S. "SANSPAREIL,"

Balaklava,

January, 1855.

MEMORANDUM RESPECTING BALAKLAVA HARBOUR.

Drawn up for the Information of Admiral Boxer.

*Piloting and Berthing.*

It is of the utmost importance that no sailing vessel should, during the winter months, remain at anchor outside the harbour. Captain Christie has established a signal post on the Eastern cliff, whence information is given respecting ships in the offing. From this post Marriott's signals are used to the ships outside, and a local code transmits the information received to Captain Christie, and to the Senior Officer in the harbour.

Commander Powell of the "Vesuvius," assisted by Mr. Reid, Master of that ship, has the entire direction of the piloting of vessels in and out of harbour, and of appointing them their berths.

For this purpose the three tug vessels "Circassia," "Varna," and "Shark," are at his disposal, but the "Varna" and "Shark," being the smallest and handiest, are in general use.

The "Minna" and "Brenda" are never used for towing, but they go alongside of vessels outside when the water is smooth, and bring in troops. Each of these two vessels will carry seven hundred or eight hundred men, or from sixty to eighty horses.

There are four troop boats and five heavy lighters belonging to the harbour, they are in charge of the Senior Officer. There is also one double boat with a platform over it, but it is not in good repair, and is generally used as a floating wharf.

To ensure clear anchors and close stowage of the vessels in port, it is absolutely necessary that the piloting and berthing should be in the hands of an experienced Officer, and that he should not be diverted from these duties.

## *Wharfage.*

The berths opposite the first open space on the Eastern side after entering the harbour are kept as much as possible for the cattle ships; the smaller ones can land their cargoes (with the assistance of light brows) directly on to the wharf, the larger ones can do so with the assistance of the double boat or floating wharf. This saves much time as the cattle walk on shore.

The next landing place is Ordnance Wharf, where shot and some descriptions of ordnance stores are usually landed. From thence up to the head of the harbour are a number of small projecting landing places, variously appropriated by the Commissariat to the different articles of provisions. Bread, rum, meat, etc., have each a place appointed to them.

The last wharf at the end of the town is solely for embarking sick. Opposite to it is a canvas building for their reception, if they should be detained whilst waiting for boats.

On the Western side of the harbour is a small plot of ground enclosed by rocks, which is the Navy dockyard, and useful for hauling up boats, storing driftwood, etc. The Engineers have a sawpit there, and are working up the large driftwood into sleepers for gun platforms.

The tugs and small steamers can go alongside the next—called the Vesuvius Wharf. All troops are disembarked there.

Sheers are erected at Diamond Wharf, and here all the guns are landed, but the water is shoal and as the large lighters cannot get up they must always be put into troop or paddle-box boats. Shells and powder are also landed here, and hay and chopped straw close to it.

### *General Duties.*

As a rule the transports land as much provisions as the Commissariat require, without assistance in men from the Royal Navy, but when more help is required a special application is made.

Mr. Drake, A. C. General, is the Officer in charge

of the provision department of the Commissariat, and it is with this gentleman that the Navy have principally to communicate.

The landing of ordnance stores is almost entirely done by the Navy, also that of horses and cattle when the vessels cannot be taken alongside a wharf. The landing of hay generally requires help, both in men and boats.

Small working parties are constantly required for improvements in the harbour, building piers, etc., and boats' crews to assist the larger vessels with hawsers when coming in or going out of harbour.

A boarding book is kept from which the length of time a vessel has been in harbour can be ascertained. There is a tendency amongst the private traders to turn their ships into retail shops, and to prevent this, notice should be given to them on arriving that they will not be allowed to remain in harbour beyond a certain day.

On the arrival of such a vessel her Master is required to sign a notice that the sale of spirits or wine except to Officers is forbidden, also a notice enjoining the utmost caution against fire; also a notice to colliers forbidding the sale of coal; and one to steamers requiring them to land all cinders on the beach to harden the roads—of all of which notices I attach copies.

Every vessel on arriving should immediately send its invoices of cargo to the department to which they are consigned, and will receive thence

## MEANS OF COMMUNICATION. 181

directions for their disposal. The Commissary-General receives the Commissariat goods. Mr. Young, Commissary of Ordnance, the ordnance stores, and Major Mackenzie, D.A.Q.M. General, the Quarter-Master General's stores. All packages for the Navy should be brought on board the Senior Officer's ship, and all for the Army should go to the private parcel office, to which an officer under Major Mackenzie has been appointed.

The "Sir Robert Sale," No. 88, is a depôt ship for provisions, etc., for the Naval Brigade, her own master and crew are on board her, and Mr. Brown, Acting-Paymaster, has charge of the provisions, etc. He victuals the Naval Brigade, and supplies clothing and monthly money both to them and the Marines. Mr. Churcher Clark has charge of the medical stores.

### *Correspondence.*

The boat signals will communicate information through successive stations to and from Head Quarters. There is regular communication between Major Mackenzie and Head Quarters by means of mounted orderlies, and letters addressed to the care of Colonel Steele, Military Secretary, can be sent by that route to the Naval Commander-in-Chief in Karatch Bay.

### *Government Stores.*

A voltaic battery with apparatus for destroying sunken ships is on board the "Queen of the South," and larger cylinders of a similar description are on board the "Ottawa." The "Ardent's" anchor and chain have been recovered near the entrance of the harbour, and are used as a stern mooring for ships berthed in that neighbourhood, and there is a large anchor belonging to the "Hydaspes" in use at present as a quarter mooring for the "Sanspareil."

L. G. HEATH,

Captain H.M.S. "Sanspareil"

and Harbour Master.

*LETTER No. 37.*

Balaklava,

April, 1855.

This is a very frightfully large sized sheet of paper for a man who intends to send a full one once a week. I must hope for the capture of Sebastopol or peace; in the one case my sheet will be easily filled, in the other I shall not have to fill it. It is nearly two months since I left, and fine weather and lots of hard work have, during that time, made a great change in the village of Balaklava. A great number of the stone houses, which had been appropriated as hospitals for the unfortunate Turks have been pulled down altogether, and turned into macadamization for the streets; for the stone houses wooden huts have been substituted. We, of course, do not expect again to have the country ankle deep in mud, and therefore these improvements (which would be great and invaluable for a next winter's campaign) must, I am afraid, be classed with the very large number of "too lates" already in the field. The new macadamization is at present rather a nuisance than otherwise.

The railroad progresses, but at a slow rate. The four miles to which it now extends have been made under most favourable circumstances of weather, but yet it has taken two months to complete it, instead of seventeen days as was expected when I left on the 1st February. I don't complain of the navvies, but if Sir John Burgoyne had been the master hand, instead of Messrs. Peto and Co., "Our Own Correspondents" would have been by this time hard at work writing him down.

Talking of "Our Own Correspondents," I dined last night with Sir Colin Campbell, and there saw a most delightful correspondence. "Our Own Correspondent" wrote to Colonel Harding, Commandant of the town, stating that he had been chased close to the French lines by Cossacks, and that having escaped them he made his way into Balaklava without once being challenged by a sentry. The letter was officially forwarded to Sir Colin Campbell, who commands the Balaklava district, and he turned it over to be answered by Stirling (known to Douglas) the Adjutant-General. The answer is most delightfully satirical, and ends with something of this sort —"You state that the gentleman in question is the correspondent of *The Times;* this gives a clue to the extraordinary exaggerations which appear in that newspaper relative to the events of the war."

General Vinois, who is Sir Colin's French neighbour, dined with us. He was present at the armistice and talked with a Russian General who said they were all very sick of it, and anxious for peace; they regretted the *bon vin de France* and were very short of cigars. A young sailor officer was just married to a "nice little English woman" and had to fight against her countrymen, and moreover was turned into a *fantassin*, neither of which arrangements did he approve of.

The general appearance of everyone is wonderfully improved. There are garrison, or rather, I believe, divisional races, both of horses and men, and I am sorry to say the English have beaten the French in running (!)—which I should not have expected. Balaklava is surrounded with huts. There is a convalescent hospital on the neighbouring heights; it consists of a series of huts containing eighteen men each, and a strong symptom of prevailing good spirits is that many of them have little gardens in front filled with transplanted wild flowers. Another striking change is that soldiers now universally salute the officers they meet—a thing never thought of when they could but just move their legs along, and had no energy left for lifting their hands to their caps. Instead of forty or fifty miserable looking mules, with no masters, there are now seventeen hundred, well looked after and cared for; they are under Colonel McMurdo, the head of the newly-established land transport corps. Then there is the railway, most useful already with its great big English cart horses, and

I don't know that I have seen anything within the last two years that has so reminded me of Old England as meeting a team of these animals, with the chain traces, swingle-tree (or whatever it is called) thrown over their backs, returning to their stables a navvy mounted sideways on the back of each, with a short pipe in his mouth and a long carter's whip over his shoulder.

There is little doubt but that the guns will open this week, and that in all probability the bombardment will be followed by an assault; with what results remains to be seen. I hear various opinions, but sanguine on the whole. There is no doubt that the Russians have lost no time, and that their ditches are both wide and deep, and it is probable that when they are passed, mines will be sprung, which will lose us men from our advanced parties, but which will make the ground the easier for those who follow. We are preparing floating hospitals for the wounded, who will not be sent away until the critical period for their wounds is passed. This day week I *hope* to write to you of Victory; and this day month you to me of consequent Peace. *Nous verrons.*

*LETTER No. 38.*

Finished, Balaklava,

April 10th, 1855.

I think I described in last week's letter my general impressions on returning to Balaklava after nearly two months' absence. I have since then had my hands pretty full, for as Captain Christie expected to have to face an inquiry on his conduct on his arrival in England, he naturally wished to take his secretary with him, and the obtaining a successor has been a longer process than I anticipated. The first to whom I offered the berth was the "Sanspareil's" clerk, but being now senior clerk in the Admiral's office he will get the first death vacancy as a paymaster, and I think wisely prefers that prospect to a mere temporary gain in income. The second one turns out to be too young to be eligible for the appointment. The third, who is appointed (Mr. Arlidge), was paymaster of the "Caradoc," and has had to settle all his own accounts with his successor before coming to me. I believe I shall have him to-morrow. He seems a very nice gentlemanly fellow which is a great point as I intend to make him my messmate; he is also said to be very hard working, which is another great point. I have had not only to write my own letters, but also to copy them into a book, and I have had to make out returns of the present employment of the transports. These were left me in a form according to the numbers of the transports. I have collected them under separate heads, so that my return gives a synoptic view of how many are employed on this duty, and how many on that. Then there is a daily report of cargo discharged by each transport which I have set going; and there is moreover a certain amount of personal visiting, etc.—all of which has employed me pretty continuously. When I catch Mr. Arlidge I shall be able to turn over the clerical work to him and take more to the active part.

I have had to fight a little with Admiral Boxer to place myself on the footing prescribed by my instructions; but I think that is all over and that we now understand one another. He is a most hard-working, zealous man, but without the slightest approach to method, and some of his work has in consequence to be done over again. If he wants a ship cleared for any particular purpose he will put all her cargo on the beach, without the slightest care as to whose charge it is to go into. I can quite conceive the confusion as to stores etc. in the Bosphorus during his reign, from hearing him report to someone, who came from Sir Edmund

Lyons to inquire, that there were only four hundred tons of coal in the harbour, when I myself (who have nothing to do with the colliers but only with the transports) know of upwards of eight hundred tons.

During the last few days a portion of the Turkish army at Eupatoria has been brought up to the camp *viâ* Kamiesh. I at first heard that ten thousand were to come, but I hear to-day the number is to be increased to twenty-five thousand. This would seem to imply that the notion of investing the north side was abandoned, and that a great push is to be made, perhaps simultaneously, on the town and on Liprandi. Deserters told us that an attack was to be made on Balaklava on Easter Day, but that has passed with no such occurrence. The officer commanding the cavalry picquet, however, had his eyes so sharpened by the report, that he sent up at daylight to head quarters to say he saw some guns mounted on what we used to call No. 3 Redoubt, opposite Balaklava. They turned out to be dark marks on the side of the hill!

Our fire opened in earnest this morning at daybreak (April 9th), and at the same time, or rather a few hours previous, the rain, which has been absent for six weeks, began to come down, and it has been pouring ever since. I suppose it is rather advantageous to us than otherwise, as it prevents Liprandi from making an attack on our end of the line, if he were so inclined. We have had but few people in from the front, but they all say that our fire is three to one superior to the Russians. I don't myself see why the Russians should fire at all; their object is to hold their own, and I think they would do that most effectually by keeping under cover, and working at repairing damages during the night with undiminished forces.

April 10th.—I have waited so long in hopes of getting some authentic news for you from the front that I have hardly time to finish my page. The latest account is that we have got the south side, but you must not make sure until you see the newspaper, for this is a shocking place for gossip.

Two o'clock.—Nothing new. The firing going on with no material result as yet. Russian fire rather stronger than yesterday.

*LETTER No. 39.*

Balaklava,

April 12th, 1855.

Your letter of March 29th has just arrived, and almost simultaneously with it the news that Captain Crofton, R.E.*, a brother of Richard in the Artillery, has lost his leg, and as I shall go to the front to-morrow morning to see what I can do for him, I had better answer you at once, rather than risk missing the mail which is made up here to-morrow evening. I read all the evidence before the Committee as reported in the *Evening Mail*, and therefore, I suppose, as reported in *The Times*. But you see the *Herald*, which I do not, and I was quite unaware that it's abuse of me still continued. We have learnt much during the war as to our commissariat, etc., but if we ever make such another war without gagging "Our Own Correspondents" at the very beginning, we shall make a greater mistake than any we have made on this occasion. I have within the last week met Sir John McNeil and also two other members of the

---

*He shortly afterwards died of his wound.

Sanitary Commission. The latter both expressed their surprise at the difference between what they found and what they expected to find. The former is carrying on his investigation very quietly, and apparently very temperately, but I find him as open to a *gobe-mouche* story as any of the Correspondents.

On his arrival here about a month ago Admiral Boxer,* who has usurped Christie's functions, ordered Sir John McNeil to be received on board an *empty* steamer called the "Gottenberg," a steamer whose hire costs £50 a day. This was the common topic of conversation, and I suppose it came to Boxer's ears, because a few days after my arrival (taking Christie's place) he took measures for transferring Sir John to a depôt ship, and the "Gottenberg" was ordered by me to England, where she and vessels of her class were much wanted. Down comes a note from General Airey to know—"Why the 'Gottenberg,' which costs less than the 'Oscar,' should be ordered home when the 'Oscar' is not?" I answer—"They are both at 50s. a ton, but one is larger than the other, one is empty and the other is full, and moreover the 'Gottenberg,' like the 'Oscar,' is hired for six months; she goes home to bring out another cargo, and if she cost twice as much as the other it

---

* Admiral Boxer was Harbour Master, and had no control over Christie, who had the complete management and direction of all the transports.

would make no difference, for whether lying here doing nothing or loading with a fresh cargo at Portsmouth she receives the same pay." It turned out that General Airey's query was founded on Sir John McNeil's representation, which was founded on the statement of the master of the "Gottenberg." I taxed Sir John with it, and pointed out it was just the sort of information on which "Our Own Correspondents'" "facts" were founded, which he admitted, but took credit to himself for sifting to the bottom at once. There are two "Arabias," the one you heard of in England is not my friend—yours was only once, that I remember, in Balaklava; the other is a sailing ship, and has been here a good deal. I think you have best advanced my interests by doing nothing. As to the "Candia," you are quite mistaken in supposing there was a shipload of medical comforts; it was merely the surplus of a supply put on board for the use of the body of troops brought from Marseilles to Kamiesh, and was very insignificant in quantity. I never took any of it; Peel may have done so in the "Diamond"—for I see Stafford makes rather a hash in his speech between our names and our ships.

As far as I have seen of the evidence before the Sebastopol Committee it strikes me as the most wonderful jumble of gossip and second editions of newspaper correspondence that has ever been gathered together before so solemn a tribunal.

The witnesses have first read *The Times*, and then (so weak is poor human nature) they have digested it until it has become (like other food) part and parcel of themselves, and they have given it to the Committee as their own opinion. *The Times* then turns round and says, " See how true our reports have been."

As to " Mr. King *versus* Captain Heath," I am inclined to let all alone until the capture of Sebastopol—which may take place to-morrow—or the Vienna conferences send me to England. Just think with what force I should come down on the Duke—" Having been absent serving under that distinguished officer, Sir Edmund Lyons, in the Crimean war, advantage has been taken by those who live at home at ease to oust me from certain privileges, etc., etc." I am very grateful to you all for going to Portsmouth to meet Mary. It will smooth her way very much, for even when she left me she was a little frightened at the thoughts of meeting you all, and your brotherly kindness will reassure her.

P.S.—I asked this evening the name of the *Herald's* Correspondent. It is Wood, and that is all I know about him.

*LETTER No. 40.*

May 5th, 1855.

The telegraph is now working in sixteen hours between this and London, but only for the Government. I have not left myself a minute's time even to thank you for your zeal in my service. The biggest "*one*" I have read in the evidence, as far as I am concerned, is told by the Master of the "Andes." He said he "managed somehow to get into this harbour and had no assistance whatever." It so happened that having taken a ship out I went on board the "Andes" outside the harbour myself, and whilst waiting for a tug I breakfasted with the Captain and then brought his vessel in. He was particularly civil, for when finally placed in safety he said "I am sure, Sir, I am very grateful to you for bringing me in, I don't know how I should have managed without you, I had no idea the place was so small and so crowded." The Captain of the "Himalaya" comes next. He was suddenly ordered to Varna on an emergency, having some charcoal on board him. He was to have returned from Varna immediately, but his engine broke down and he was obliged to go to Constantinople, instead of returning with what he had been sent for and the charcoal. All this part he leaves out in his evidence and gives the Committee to understand he was ordered with the charcoal to Varna and thence to Constantinople.

*LETTER No. 41.*

H.M.S. "Triton,"

Finished, Balaklava,

May 7th, 1855.

It is no use making excuses for the past, and I suppose my best plan is to behave better in future and write more regularly. But, besides the pressure of business, I may also plead that when one knows the electric telegraph carries its news to you in sixteen hours, one feels that an historical or political journal, like that which I have been in the habit of writing to you, must have lost a good deal of its interest by the time it reaches you. By dint of hard work we got an expedition off on Thursday evening, the 3rd instant; it consisted of about two thousand Infantry, besides some Marines from the fleet who were to land, six guns with their Artillerymen, and fifty Cavalry. The baggage horses for this force consisted of about six hundred and forty, and I believe if the expedition had not been much hurried still more would have come.

Colonel McMurdo, the Director of Land Transport, told me he had put in as many carts as possible in order to save putting in horses. He had eighty-three carts. If two thousand five hundred men require the attendance of so much transport, one cannot be surprised that it is estimated that this army of thirty thousand English must have twenty-six thousand baggage animals before it can safely leave the coast. This gives a plainer idea of the gigantic expenses attendant on a state of war and the difficulty of assuring success than anything I ever heard of. What a fine field for Cossack enterprise would such a train of animals afford. These twenty-six thousand beasts would require ten thousand cavalry to protect them, I should think! Sir Charles Trevelyan was certainly right in saying Admiral Boxer had not the administrative faculty. I found passive disobedience the only plan to adopt; and when a satisfactory arrangement had once been made I merely ignored all his attempts to disarrange it. We had some very desperate skirmishes during the day on the subject of this embarkation, and at one time he almost succeeded in driving one of my ships out of the harbour with only half a cargo, but I brought up all my reserves and carried the day. He certainly bears no malice, or else forgets what has happened, for although he must have been much annoyed at my resistance to him we are now the best of friends.

## A PROMISING "COUP" SPOILED.

May 6th.—Conceive my astonishment this morning at seeing the whole fleet returned. It seems that a thick fog prevailed all Friday and the ships had all separated, but that at daylight on the Saturday morning every one was at the appointed rendezvous a few miles from Cape Takli (near Kertch), on a beautiful calm day, most favourable for landing. The signal was made from the "Royal Albert" for all Captains, and Sir Edmund read a copy of a letter received by the French Commander from General Canrobert, stating that he had received a telegraphic despatch from Paris dated May 3rd, and the French were *positively* to return immediately. The English alone were not strong enough to undertake the thing by themselves, and moreover a number of the French troops were on board the English line of battle ships. So here they are back again. It is said that the French force was short by a battery of Artillery and fifteen hundred Infantry of what they had promised. The strangest part of the business is that Canrobert does not seem to have communicated this despatch to Lord Raglan.

May 7th.—There is nothing to add to the above. Canrobert has spoiled one of the most promising *coups* that could have been.* The Kertch forts taken, our ships could have held the Straits, and our steam gun boats once inside would, I suppose, have been more than a match for anything there,

---

* Vide Page 201.

and the Sea of Azov, which I fancy is the high road by which Sebastopol's provisions principally travel, would have been ours. However, there is an end to it, and I suppose the *entente cordiale* will suffer. We have been regularly sauntering over the whole business of landing the force. It is such disheartening work—everything was promising, weather calm, a capital chart made by Spratt of the "Spitfire," the Russians alarmed by a demonstration previously made at Loujah and Anapa, etc., etc.

Some of the Sardinians have arrived at Constantinople, but wait there for General Marmora. It is a good thing to have got even a portion of them, as it fixes them politically. Another regiment of cavalry arrived, the 12th Lancers from India, and remount horses for the Artillery are pouring in. Provisions and stores of all kinds are abundant, and the new advanced batteries with much heavier guns than the last time are nearly ready for opening. I wish you would send Louis Napoleon out to us, and then I think the business might be settled as far as the south side is concerned. That done, and the fine weather allowing us to use the beach, the north side might be regularly invested.

First Expedition to Kertch.

(*Vide* Letter No. 41).

My Dear Heath,

I am sorry since I received Sir Charles Wood's last letter that we have sent anything home lately excepting the "Simla" and "Jason." We must not send anything more without an absolute necessity for so doing.

I can assure you that I am very sensible of the exertions you must have made to equip the expedition so quickly and so well, and I am much obliged to you for it.

Yours faithfully,

E. Lyons.


R.A., May 7th, 1855.

How is war to be carried on if it depends upon Canrobert's interpretation of telegraphic messages?

*LETTER No. 42.*

Balaklava,

May 8th, 1855.

I shall be very glad to get the Sebastopol Blue Book. The dead cows were naturally my business, as I had charge of the harbour, but I agreed with Christie that he should look after them, and I pressed on him that he should make the hospital ships take the whole business of removing them in regular weekly turns. However, he preferred that every ship should tow out those that were near her, and, as what is everybody's business never is done by anyone, so every ship trusted to the animals drifting away from them before being found out. Commander Gordon might prove how frequently boats were out collecting wood, and Dacres might clearly place the blame of more not having been collected on Lord Raglan's shoulders, for he officially declined it when Dacres officially offered to collect it. I thought I had mentioned before that it was on the 11th and not the 13th I was called in by Dacres to help him in the harbour work.

## LETTER No. 43.

Balaklava,

May 26th, 1855.

The great event of the day is our change of masters—Pellissier *vice* Canrobert. Everyone is in spirits about it, and glad to get an energetic man as Commander-in-Chief to do something with the two hundred thousand troops there must now be under him in the Crimea. The strange part of the business is that Canrobert, instead of retiring to his country house, remains out as General of Division under Bosquet, who commands a Corps d'Armée. One cannot conceive the possibility of Lord Raglan changing places with Sir G. Browne, or Sir Edmund Lyons with Admiral Boxer! Greater energy is already shown. The Kertch expedition revived was the first thing—I got intimation of it on Sunday evening the 20th, we got it officially the next day and started most of them off on Tuesday evening, and by dint of working all night the last left us on Wednesday morning at 7 o'clock. Three thousand Infantry, six guns, fifty Cavalry, and one thousand horses (which includes Artillery, Cavalry, and everything) was the English contingent. Five thousand Turks, and seven thousand French embarked from Kamiesh.* I reckon Sir Edmund Lyons and Sir George Browne worth one or two thousand more but I don't know who is in command of the expedition. The weather has been very favourable and we expect to-day to hear of their having landed.

Yesterday at daylight an advance was made by about twenty-five thousand French and Turks to the ground where the battle of Balaklava was fought, in front of Balaklava as far as the Tchernaya. They are regularly encamped and intend to live there. Whether this movement is made merely to make room for newcomers, or whether it is to feel the way for a further advance, I don't know. I rode out last night to the new lines, every one looked free, and it was pleasant even to me to gallop over a grassy plain that I have only been able to look at for so long. The wild flowers around Balaklava are more beautiful than any I have ever seen, and the new ground is covered with them. You know I am not learned in their names, so I can only tell you that their colours are of the most brilliant and varied hues, and some of them very beautiful and delicate in shape. There are some thistles so elegant in form that the most hungry donkey would pause to admire before he stooped to eat!—I don't think even a

---
* Vide Page 206.

country gentleman with his spud could help sparing them.

Our remounts of Artillery and Cavalry are coming out fast; Sardinians are pouring in; ordnance stores of all sorts, powder, shot, shell, etc., are daily arriving. The troops are fed in the most luxurious manner, except in the article of beef, which is the most wretchedly lean miserable-looking stuff conceivable. I suppose as the season advances bullocks will get fat. Fresh bread has been brought from Constantinople for some time; a bakery is now established at Kadikoi, and another has been sent out fitted in a small ship.

Mr. Soyer is busy organising kitchens. I have seen a good deal of him; he is exceedingly egotistical, but has all the marks of a great man in his own line. His conversation is all about his work; he soars beyond mere sauces and ragouts, but goes into the expense of different markets and different sorts of food, and examines whether fresh vegetables from Constantinople are or are not better than compressed ones from France. He has given me a recipe for making ship's beef and pork delicious, and says if he could have had his way it would (five or six years ago) have been preserved with far less salt than at present, and would not have cost a bit more or been more liable to decay. There is a little cholera in the camp and there have been a few cases down here, but it does not increase.

## Second Expedition to Kertch.

R.A. Strait of Kertch,

June 2nd, 1855.

My Dear Heath,

I am very much gratified by your hearty congratulations, and so will Jack\* be I am very sure. His success has been very great. In four days two hundred and forty-seven vessels employed in carrying supplies to the Crimea captured and destroyed. —Four steamers of war under the command of Rear Admiral Woolf run in here, burnt to the water's edge and destroyed by the enemy.

Arabat's principal powder magazine blown up. Two immense magazines of corn and flour destroyed by the squadron at Bormarsand and Gonithreiste, containing two months rations for a hundred thousand men. I have sent him two ship's launches to enable him to do as much damage as possible to the enemy in the neighbourhood of Taganrog.

Here we find more than a hundred guns, many of them of heavy calibre and beautifully cast. The day of our approach the enemy destroyed here a large magazine of corn and flour, which, taken

---

\* "Jack" was Sir Edmund's sailor son. He commanded the "Miranda," and shortly after this successful raid he was sent in to one of our naval night *alertes* off Sebastopol, where his leg was shot off, and he died, regretted by all who knew him, in the hospital at Constantinople.

## SIR EDMUND LYONS' SAILOR SON. 207

together with what was destroyed in the Sea of Azof, comprised four months rations for a hundred thousand men.

The firing cases of combustibles in the passages and entrances broken in the Forts with the connecting wires attached; and in the dockyard are fifty-seven more cases quite ready to be sunk. The enemy fired upon our ships, not believing that we had a soldier to spare from the siege.

I am very glad that you have transports to send for Vivian's and Beaton's troops. What a blessing that the fire was put out in the "Manilla."

Yours very faithfully,
E. LYONS.

*LETTER No. 44.*

Balaklava,

Finished, July 14th, 1855.

What with writing to Admiralty, Transport Board, Admirals, General, and wife, brothers and sisters have certainly been neglected. I don't think I even added a page to the book of journals on the sad 18th June, nor have I mentioned the death of Admiral Boxer of cholera, or that Lord Raglan died on the 28th June of acute diarrhœa, aggravated probably by grief for the ill-success of the 18th. Lord Raglan was a perfect specimen of the English gentleman, and a high-minded chivalrous soldier; his rank and courteous bearing did much to maintain the *entente cordiale*. General Simpson, the Chief of the Staff, became the new Commander-in-Chief. The events of the 18th June are never spoken of without an accompanying holding up of hands, and an exclamation that "there never was so ill-managed a business." There are complaints of the want of instruction as to what was intended; want of proper directions to the covering parties and reserves; want of numbers in the assaulting columns ; and the absence of all feints or attempts at diversions. That the last would have been useful is evident from the fact (of which I believe there is no doubt) that General Eyres would, if supported, have had the Flagstaff Battery and all that part of the town. He did not go (whether by accident or design I don't know) to the place to which he was intended to go, and found his way in where a way was not suspected ; but, however good the arrangements might have been, I fancy success would have been impossible, for our assaulting columns had to cross seven or eight hundred yards of ground open to crossfire of grape shot from numerous flanking batteries. Drop the curtain !

Since the 18th enormous quantities of ammunition have been sent up to the front. We have advanced a certain distance towards the Redan, and the French a greater distance towards the Malakoff, and they have nearly completed a battery at the head of the careering creek, from which wonders are expected.

The few criticisms I have heard on the new Commander-in-Chief are all favourable, but to-day it is reported that the electric telegraph has named some one to succeed him. Admiral Freemantle has not yet appeared, although some letters and newspapers have arrived to his address, nor have I heard a line on the subject from Sir Edmund.

Hamilton has gone away on three weeks' leave of absence, and I am left alone in my glory. I shall find out what my real position in the regular service is, for I find Hamilton has left orders with his senior lieutenant to consider himself the Senior Officer of H.M. Ships. I have made myself so for the present, and referred to Sir Edmund.*

The railroad people are all adrift and are about to return to England, I don't think they prove much for the Administrative Reformers. The men are very discontented and disorganised. One waggon goes about with—"The driver of this ain't 'ad no wages for six months and not much wittals." The road itself is likely to be very shaky in the winter, and I hope for the harbour of Sebastopol, or else that large stores shall be made beforehand up in front—at which there is as yet no attempt, and July is drawing on. Those knowing French are said to have persuaded Omer Pasha and ourselves to come out of the Baidar valley, "being too far in the advance and being unhealthy," and as soon as the ground was clear their own cavalry marched in and are heaping up immense supplies of forage. The story is so characteristic that it is a pity I cannot say I think there is no exaggeration in it. I have no domestic news. I have got a turtle swimming about, tied to the ship, waiting to adorn my dinner to the new Admiral when he comes.

---

*Sir Edmund decided that having no pendant flying I could not take military command, and Sir Houston Stewart agreed with him.

My farmyard does not prosper; the hens give me no eggs. My new horse is splendid, but I cannot sell the old one; prices are much fallen.

---

R.A., June 7th, 1855.

My Dear Heath,

I am much shocked at the sudden death of poor Admiral Boxer; but it is a comfort to me to feel that I may have sweetened the last days of his life by promoting his son.

I have written to Sir Charles Wood to say that, in my opinion, it would be a mistake to appoint anyone senior to you to Balaklava.

Yours sincerely,

E. Lyons.

## LETTER No. 45.

Finished, Balaklava,
September 11th, 1855.

Had I begun my journal on the day of the final attack on Sebastopol (the 8th September) I should have written in a very melancholy mood; and even now that success has crowned the Allied Arms, and that the great prize which has cost so much has become ours, my rejoicing is very very much sobered by the dark cloud which obscures the glories of Alma and Inkerman. However, I had better begin at the beginning. The bombardment was much heavier than usual for a day or two before the 8th, but it was taken up only occasionally and was not continuous.

On the 7th the order was confidentially issued that an attack was to be made on the 8th, and as I heard of it I went to the front to see it. Noon was the appointed hour for the French to attack the Malakoff, and so soon as they had obtained *un succès assuré* they were to show an English ensign from the Mamelon and we were to attack the Redan. The day was very windy, so much so that the fleet which was to have helped could not move from their anchors, and it was very dusty, which

## CAPTURE OF MAMELON.

rather prevented our seeing well, for the wind was in our faces. I went first to Cathcart's hill, but at half past eleven crossed over to the next hill on the right, whence I saw more of the Malakoff but rather less of the Redan. Almost precisely at noon the French moved out and entered the Malakoff without a check, and from the first moment of their advance one continuous stream of men was poured in for a full half hour or more.

They seem to have taken the Russians quite by surprise, for as far as I can hear there was next to no resistance made to them at that point, which being the highest spot in the place was the key to the whole thing. In the rear of the Malakoff were the ruined huts of part of the town, to which such Russians as were in the place retreated, and where fresh bodies joined them, and sheltered by these ruins they continued the whole afternoon to try and regain their loss, but without success. The French were also engaged until night in attempting what is called the Little Redan, which is to the right (as we look at it) of the Malakoff; but there they were unsuccessful, and of that attack I saw nothing and have not heard much, but the musketry firing was very heavy the whole afternoon.

The signal was made from the Mamelon almost immediately after the French attack began, and our assaulting party went out of the trenches well enough, but although they got into the Redan and were followed by the supports as far as the parapet, the men would go no further and allowed themselves to be driven back again by (I am told) not more than two hundred Russians, who chased them out and pelted them down the parapet with stones. Sir William Codrington and General Markham commanded the assault, and the latter is said to have positively refused to send on the reserves. It must have required some courage to refuse, but I think General Markham was quite right in doing so. After lying about under the cover of the parapet and in the ditch for perhaps an hour, the survivors of the assaulting party and supports made their way back as best they could to the trenches, and thus ended the 8th September.

During the night some of the men from the advanced trenches were bringing in wounded, and gradually got nearer and nearer to the Redan, which seeming unusually quiet they at last looked in at an embrasure and found the place evacuated. A succession of explosions in the town and a number of fires confirmed the good news, and at daylight the mastheads only of the line of battle ships were to be seen above water, and the floating bridge was cut in two, whether by accident or design we do not know.

I rode up in the middle of the day and, providing myself with a pass from head quarters, took a walk in Sebastopol. Five squadrons of cavalry had been sent out to prevent anyone going in without passes,

## A WALK IN SEBASTOPOL.

but by bye-ways which were unknown to the dragoons, but which to those who had spent the last few months in the trenches were beaten tracks, all sorts of French, Sardinians, and English got in, and there could not have been fewer than five thousand there when I arrived. I went in by the ravine leading into Dockyard Creek, and walked up a road to the left of and parallel to it, getting thus into the heart of the best part of the town. Between the Dockyard Creek and the sea is another smaller creek called in the maps Artillery Creek. This creek is the mouth of a valley which divides that part of the town into two ridges, so that standing, as I did, on the edge of the higher ridge of the two I could see at one view the greater part of that quarter of the town, and although I looked very carefully I did not see a single roof without a shot hole in it, whilst many were entirely destroyed. Pieces of shells cover the paths in all directions, and I think the total loss suffered by the Russians from beginning to end must have been something unthought of hitherto. There are no really good houses, and the only public building I saw of any pretensions was a stone imitation of the Temple of Theseus at Athens. The other houses are all plastered, and the doors and windows flimsy and thin.

There was not a house to be seen without its English, or more generally French, ransackers, but there was little left for plunderers beyond a few tables, chairs, and wardrobes, some of which were carried off, but most of them wantonly broken up and destroyed for amusement. A splendid brass bell took the fancy of the French, and as one Zouave got tired of pulling at it another succeeded him. They discovered what seemed to have been an hotel or club-house with a large store of drinkables, which had the effect of making the mob more noisy whilst I was coming out than when I first went in. I brought away some seeds which I took from some flowers in a garden attached to what we have always called the Admiralty, and also the drawings for building a boat which I found with a great many others of the same sort in a house which must have been that of the Surveyor of the Navy. Fort Paul blew up whilst I was in the town, and several minor explosions took place, at which several plunderers were burnt. I retraced my steps after this, and going round the head of Dockyard Creek climbed up a steep hill into the Redan.

You probably know that the Redan is built on the crest of a spur, on which same spur is our right attack, or twenty-one gun battery. I cannot describe to you the state of the ground behind the parapet; it was dimpled all over by the bursting of our shells—there did not seem over the whole space to be a single square yard untouched. The parapet was enormously thick, and the guns were all or nearly all mounted and in good order,

INTERIOR OF THE REDAN.
September, 1855.

which I was surprised to see, for we have heard so much of their guns being continually dismounted that I expected to see a complete wreck.

I have heard it given as a reason for our discomfiture on the 8th that another line of works faced our assaulting party as soon as they had surmounted the parapet. There was nothing of the sort. The ditch may originally have been deep, but the constant fire on the parapet has crumbled it away, and there is now nothing for an assailant to do but to go down about four feet into the ditch and then climb up, or rather scramble up, a parapet no steeper than a steep hill. No ladders are requisite. There is nothing behind the parapet at the angle which was assaulted, but there is a massive longitudinal traverse built parallel to the parapet immediately behind the guns on each face of the angle— intended, I presume, to save the gunners from the bursting of shells behind them. I had no time to go on further, but hope to get another day to see the dockyard and the Malakoff.

The evacuation has been well managed. I don't hear of any prisoners, except those taken by the French on the 8th, nor of any stores of provisions having been found; indeed, I have heard of nothing but anchors, guns, and shot, of which there are still large numbers quite new and untouched. An allied commission is to take account of the public property, and the police of the town is given over to the French.

*LETTER No. 46.*

Finished, Balaklava,

September 14th, 1855.

Wonders will never cease, and here is the latest in the shape of a second journal letter in one week. But Sebastopol does not fall every day, and my last was written too much in a shamefaced spirit to be allowed to remain alone. I went yesterday to head quarters intending to get a pass, but finding Sir Edmund, Sir Houston, etc. etc., all collected there and about to visit the same places I wished to see, *viz.*, the Malakoff and the dockyard, I joined their party. As might, however, have been expected, when Admirals Bruat and Lyons were in a carriage we equestrians managed to miss them, and Sir Houston and myself were left to ourselves.

We entered the town through the net work of trenches (a roadway having been filled up already) opposite the valley which terminates in Artillery Creek and close to the Russian left of Flagstaff Battery, or the Bastion du Mât. Thence we went rambling through the same part of the town which

## A SIGHT WORTH SEEING.

I had visited the previous time, then round the head of Dockyard Creek, in rear of the Redan into the Malakoff. Here it was lucky I was with the Admiral, for no one was admitted under the rank of a General Officer, and the visit was well worth the trouble. Todleben should have been a railway contractor. The dream of moving such masses of earth as are piled up in all directions, to shelter the soldiers as much as possible from shells, and of digging such ditches, and forming so massive a parapet, could hardly have entered any one's head but that of a Brassey or Peto. The sight is quite wonderful, and the more so from the knowledge that it was all done (as I heard a French Officer remark) *sous notre nez*. The remains of the original White Tower are piled round with earth, and some sixty Russians with an Officer held it and kept all assailants at bay for two hours after the place had been taken. There was but one small door and two or three loopholes from which they shot down all who came near. They ultimately surrendered, otherwise I suppose Pellissier might have tried his old plan upon them.

The French got in to the Malakoff by surprise, and indeed as their advanced trench was quite close up to the ditch they always had that chance open to them, for the continual shelling, with small mortars firing small charges, must have made it quite impossible to keep anything like a mass of troops always there ready to repel an assault—and it strikes me that this faculty of working close up to a fortification, and then choosing your own time for an assault, is the real reason that a fortress even such as the Malakoff must eventually fall. There is a clever article in the *Edinburgh Review* on Modern Fortification, but the author has left out this fact in his discussion. Although I am very sore, not so much at our own repulse as at the reason of it, there seems no doubt that our attack did good service, and I have heard it stated that Pellissier said, "But for the diversion you made, and the mass of troops the Russians were in consequence obliged to keep in the Redan all the afternoon for fear of a renewal of the assault, I could not have held my ground." The French were themselves repulsed with great loss at the Little Redan.

From the Malakoff I went to the Mamelon, and then to the dockyard, through a mass of ruins. In this quarter of the town, as in that which I described in my last, not a house can be seen untouched. The fine storehouses which line the Dockyard Creek are the most untouched; these had been turned into hospitals and I am told that a Russian steamer with a flag of truce carried off all that were alive and that there were left only three or four hundred dead—whom we had to bury; the process was going on while I passed.

The famous docks disappointed me much—judging by the eye I don't think anything larger

## SEBASTOPOL DOCKS.

than a small frigate could get in. There is but one entrance to five docks; the breadth of that entrance

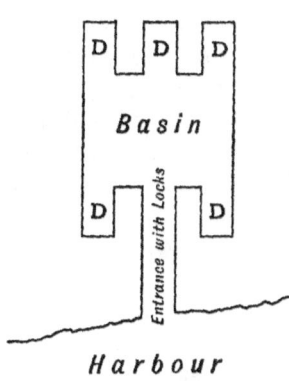

of course governs the others. You probably know that to save immense excavations these docks are built above the level of the harbour and are filled with fresh water from the Tchernaya. They are now empty, perhaps the garrison have been living on the water. I believe no stores of any consequence have been found in the place, so that when our prize money is divided amongst two hundred thousand men none of us will get much, unless we sell the docks to a joint stock company under the new Limited Liability Act! A Joint Commission has been appointed to look after and take a list of the property—Drummond is our naval commissioner. The Russians are working away at more earth works on the north side, we fire a few shells to disturb them. It is the general opinion that neither English nor French armies would make another trench to save their lives; the rejoicing at having done with them for the present is universal.

### WIND UP.

Sebastopol having fallen, and Admiral Fremantle having hoisted his flag in Balaklava Harbour, with instructions to take over not only the charge of the harbour but also of the transports, I thought I might fairly attempt to return to the regular line—more particularly as I had recently discovered that my service with the transports did not count for sea time, and I therefore applied for permission to return home. I spent about six weeks more in Balaklava, explaining all there was to explain to the Admiral, and I left for England in November, 1855. In the following month I was given command of the "Seahorse" screw mortar ship, intended for the bombardment of Cronstadt; but peace having happily been made in the Spring of 1856, I took part in the great Naval Review, and then made a trip to my old haunts to help in bringing back the army.

Thus ended my Crimean War experiences.

L. G. HEATH.

*May*, 1897.

# APPENDIX.

January 20 1835

My dear Captain Beaufort

Many thanks for your
letter of to day.

The books were certainly
bought on the suggestion
of Mr Gilbert and he does
not like to give up what
he considers his property
for the discharge of a
fictitious branch of the
publick service, but
I think I shall be able
to make a satisfactory
arrangement

I have informed Hamilton

that you have now covers for eighty will have eighty more tomorrow and will complete the accommodation for the whole number in two or three days more

I have desired Dr. Wall and Captain Keats to visit the Village of [Cairné?] and fix upon an eligible spot for a hut hospital. If they find one, it would not be difficult to convey [them?] that short distance

Should this arrangement be made only the

Admiral Dundas
Carpenters for the Ships.
yours faithfully
Raglan

7 H. S. Thursday

My Dear [illegible]

The Friend [illegible] has asked me [illegible] Action off — [illegible] you [illegible] — we have come [illegible] quickly.

The Launch of Vengeance [illegible] you — [illegible] — Remember one thing — [illegible] Nelson [illegible] out — [illegible] Cables are [illegible]

[illegible handwritten text]

## Translation of the Facsimile of Admiral Dundas's Letter.

½ past 5, Thursday.

The French Admiral has asked me to get "Caton" off. I send you to do this, as I am sure it will be done well and quickly. The Launch of "Vengeance" I send with you. Victual them. Remember one thing—Steamers can never pull vessels off shore. Get your anchor out. Lighten her *after the cables are taut*, and I have no fear of the result.

I do not like to interfere in "Friedland's" case, but if I am right they are going on a foolish plan of trying all their steam power to get her off. It must be with anchors *in the ground!* If you have an opportunity say so to the Vice-Admiral.

When you are done with "Caton" call on b$^{d.}$ V.-Adm$^{l.}$ Desfosses and offer your services—but don't press them—but return here.

Y$^{rs.}$ sincerely,

J. W. D. DUNDAS.

## APPENDIX.

### Translation of the Facsimile of Sir Edmund Lyons's Letter.

"Royal Albert,"
Off Sebastopol,
May 2nd, 1855.

My Dear Heath,

I think it very desirable to take the "Witley Park" with me in order that I may have the advantage of the local knowledge of her Commander, so you may take out of her and put into her whatever you may consider best between this and Friday evening, when I hope the French may have embarked all their troops, etc., etc. I am not without hopes of getting away to-morrow evening, but even in that case the next evening would do for the departure of the "Witley Park" if it should be found convenient to retain her.

We are told that there are rockets in the "Orient." If so we should like to have them. I am going to Head Quarters and intend to remain there until half-past four or a quarter to five o'clock.

Whatever you do look out and send all the brows and gang-boards for the paddle-box boats that you can find, and the steamer should tow round five of the Malta flat bottom boats.

Y$^{rs.}$ faithfully,

Ed$^{D.}$ Lyons.

The vessels will all be off the harbour at daylight to-morrow morning and send in their paddle-box boats for the troops.

Royal Alhambra, Upper [illegible]
                 Jan 2 - 1875

My dear [Hunter?]

         I think it very desirable
to take the [Kitty Parker?] with me
in order that I may know the
advantages of her head handle
& her [commendation?] if [you] can
take out [for] hour & [push?] into hour
whatever you may consider [to be]
between this & Friday Evening when
                                                I

[illegible handwritten letter]

[illegible handwritten letter]

## Order of Sailing of the Combined Squadrons.

The two Squadrons will generally sail in two columns.*

The English Column on the *Right* of the French Squadron. The French Steamers to keep a good distance on the *Left* of their Squadron, and the English Steamers a good distance on the *Right* of their Squadron. Thus placed, the Steamers offer a double advantage; they can repeat the signals of the two lines, and be ready immediately to execute the orders of their Admirals: their distance abreast of their squadrons should be such that always following the movements of their columns they may not in any way impede or endanger them. This will be the more easy being always under steam (the French Steamers at least).

Should the Order of Sailing in one line be adopted, the French Admiral, being always at the head of his Squadron, will be in the centre of the line if the English Squadron takes the lead under the direction of its own Admiral.

The Steamers will then continue to keep always abreast of their Squadrons, and as much as possible to windward.

---

* By night the columns will be about two miles apart.

## Order of Battle.

The Order of Battle must alike be according to circumstances: The Order in one or two columns.

The following propositions are made to provide for the principal cases should a meeting occur with the Enemy's Forces and to ensure a common action to both Squadrons.

1st.—The Enemy's Squadron is signalized to Leeward in Line of Battle: the Combined Fleet is ranged to Windward in a Single Line.

On the signal to bear up together, each of the Ships of the Combined Fleet will by degrees, steer, so as to place themselves abreast of the Enemy's Vessels, or, if it be wished to cut the Line, the leading ships will steer—so as to reach the Enemy's third ship before the centre, and all the Combined Fleet arriving thus on a part of the Enemy's Line, will employ against them a numerical superiority of force, whether their vessels take a position abreast of the Enemy's Line, or whether they cut it, and place between two fires its Centre and Rear Ships.

2nd.—The Enemy's Squadron is signalized to Windward and in Line of Battle: The Combined Fleet is ranged to Leeward in One Line.

The Fleet is to be beat to Windward so as to steer on the opposite tack towards the centre of the Enemy's Line; they may thus either cut the Enemy's Line, or defile towards its extremity, and place its rear "Hors de Combat," but in general they will not commence action to Leeward except on the opposite Tack.

3rd.—The Enemy's Squadron is signalled to Leeward and in Line of Battle: the Combined Fleet is ranged to Windward in two columns.

On the Signal to bear up, each of the Admirals in Chief in the columns steer to cut the Enemy's Line to place the Centre and Rear between two Fires with so much the more chance of success that the wind is favourable to them.

4th.—The Enemy's Squadron is signalized to Windward and in Line of Battle: the Combined Fleet is ranged to Leeward in two columns, steering on the opposite Tack.

If it be wished to attack in this order, it must beat to Windward so that the column most to Windward may steer to cut the third ship before the centre of the Enemy's Line; and the column to Leeward, towards the Centre of the Rear. The Action of the two columns will then concentrate with superior force towards a part only of the Enemy's Squadron; but from a position to Leeward, the attack by two columns is very difficult.

5th.—If, in conclusion, the Enemy's Fleet is signalized at Anchor with Springs, on their Cables, and the Combined Fleet decide to attack them there, they will adopt if possible, in engaging them at anchor, the same mode of attack as that which was chosen in engaging them under sail: thus the

Combined Fleet will steer so as to envelope if possible, the Centre and Van of the Enemy's Line, in case the Van and Centre are head to wind and current; and on the contrary to surround their Centre and Rear, if the Rear should be to Windward of the said Line.

It will follow that the part of the Enemy's Fleet not attacked, finding themselves placed to Leeward of the Group of Combatants, could not without difficulty and great delay render them help.

With regard to the Steamers, their part is to keep under shelter of their Ships, so as to be able to take them in tow if necessary, to man prizes, and carry the orders of the Admirals, and to take a favourable position.

(Signed)  J. W. D. DUNDAS,
*Vice-Admiral.*


GENERAL AFTER ORDER.

Head Quarters before Sebastopol,

December 13th, 1854.

The Commander of the Forces has great satisfaction in publishing copies and extracts of despatches which he has received from His Grace the Duke of Newcastle, Minister-at-War, announcing the Queen's gracious approbation of the conduct of the Army, and the Royal Navy and Marines, in co-operation with the Troops; and expressing Her Majesty's sympathy in the sufferings of the wounded of both Services, and her deep regret for the loss of the Soldiers and Sailors who have fallen in the late operations.

---

No. 152.

War Department,

November 20th, 1854.

MY LORD,

I have the honour to acknowledge the receipt of your Lordship's despatches Nos. 83 and 84, of the 18th and 23rd of October.

I have submitted to the Queen the interesting reports with which your Lordship has furnished me, in these despatches, of the commencement and subsequent progress of those vast operations in which the Allied Armies and Fleets of Her Majesty and of the Emperor of the French, in conjunction with those of the Sultan, are engaged against the stronghold of their common enemy; and I am commanded by Her Majesty to express to your Lordship, and, through you, to the Army under your command, the high satisfaction with which she has received the intelligence, no less of the very effective manner in which the fire of the allied batteries was opened, than of the energy and determination with which the fire was subsequently sustained. The unfortunate occurrence of the explosion of a Magazine in one of the French batteries, which took place at an early stage of the operations, must doubtless have prevented any immediate effect of a decisive nature being produced on the enemy's works; but Her Majesty rejoices to find that the energetic and persevering efforts of the French Commander enabled him to overcome the temporary check which this disaster appears to have imposed upon the exertions of the forces under his command.

Her Majesty is fully sensible of the motives which induced your Lordship to secure the co-operation of the Combined Fleets in the attack upon the enemy's works at the mouth of the harbour simultaneously with the fire from the batteries on the land side. The aid which, so far as they were enabled to render it, was thus afforded by the Naval, to the exertions of the Land Forces, is highly appreciated by Her Majesty; and I am further commanded to express the gratification with which Her Majesty has received the intelligence communicated by you of the able and gallant assistance afforded by the Sailors from the Fleet, under the command of Captain Lushington and Captain Peel, in the Land Batteries.

Her Majesty deeply sympathises with those who, during the progress of the operations which form the subject of your present despatches, have been wounded in the service of their Country, and has received with sincere sorrow your report of the loss of those of her gallant Soldiers and Sailors who have been killed.  It is impossible that operations of such great magnitude and difficulty—more especially when the vast resources of the enemy and his powerful means of resistance are taken into consideration—should be unattended by loss; and Her Majesty cannot but rejoice that, under the continued exposure to the incessant fire of an enemy vastly superior in numbers, to which Her Forces, both Naval and Military, have been subjected, that loss, during the period included in the Returns of Casualties enclosed in your despatches, is not so great as might have been anticipated.

I have the honour to be,

My Lord,

Your Lordship's most obedient humble Servant,

NEWCASTLE.

Field-Marshal
  THE LORD RAGLAN, G.C.B.,
    Etc., etc., etc.

## APPENDIX.

### Extract of a Letter from the Duke of Newcastle to Lord Raglan.

Dated, November 21st, 1854.

"I take the present opportunity to assure your Lordship of the satisfaction with which I have received the testimony borne by Major-General Sir Colin Campbell, in his report enclosed in your despatch of the 28th of October, to the assistance rendered by the Royal Marine Artillery and Royal Marines in opposing the advance of the Enemy's Cavalry in the Action before Balaklava of the 25th of that month."

---

War Department,
23rd November, 1854.

My Lord,

I have the honour to acknowledge the receipt of your Lordship's despatch, No. 94, of the 31st of October, which reached me on the 17th instant.

I have lost no time in submitting to the Queen the names of those Officers whom Lieutenant-General the Earl of Lucan considers as entitled to be specially mentioned for their services in the Action of the 25th of October in front of Balaklava, and whom your Lordship commends to my notice; and I have received Her Majesty's commands to desire that your Lordship will convey to each of the Officers in question the high approbation with which Her Majesty has viewed their valour and excellent conduct in that Action.

I have the honour to be,

My Lord,

Your Lordship's most obedient humble Servant,

NEWCASTLE.

Field Marshal

THE LORD RAGLAN, G.C.B.,

By order (Signed) J. B. B. ESTCOURT Adj.-General.

---

## GENERAL ORDERS.

Head Quarters, before Sebastopol,

December 24th, 1854.

The Commander of the Forces has the greatest satisfaction in publishing to the Army two despatches from the Minister of War, the one expressing the Queen's entire approbation of the conduct of the Troops at the battle of Inkerman, the other signifying Her Majesty's gracious intention of conferring a Medal upon all the Officers and Soldiers of the Army who have been engaged in the arduous and brilliant campaign in the Crimea.

The Commander of the Forces congratulates the Army on receiving so distinguished a mark of Her Majesty's favour and high appreciation of their gallant exertions; and he deems it his duty at the same time to draw the particular attention of all to the following passage in the Duke of Newcastle's despatch of the 27th instant:—"Let not any private soldier in the ranks believe that his conduct is unheeded—the Queen thanks him—his Country honours him."

---

War Department,
November 27th, 1854.

MY LORD,

I received on the 22nd instant your Lordship's despatch of the 8th of this month, communicating the intelligence of the glorious battle of the 5th, in which a determined attack by vastly superior numbers of the Enemy was completely repulsed by the unfaltering steadiness and gallantry of the Allied Armies. I immediately laid before the Queen the details of this important victory, and it is now my grateful duty to express to your Lordship Her Majesty's high appreciation of the noble exertions of her Troops in a conflict which is unsurpassed in the annals of war for persevering valour and chivalrous devotion. The strength and fury of the attacks, repeatedly renewed by fresh columns with a desperation which appeared to be irresistible, were spent in vain against the unbroken lines and the matchless intrepidity of the men they had to encounter. Such attacks could only be repulsed by that cool courage, under circumstances the most adverse, and that confidence of victory which have ever animated the British Army.

The banks of the Alma proved that no advantages of position can withstand the impetuous assault of the Army under your command. The heights of Inkerman have now shown that the dense columns of an entire army are unable to force the ranks of less than one-fourth their numbers in the hand-to-hand encounters with the bayonet which characterised this bloody day.

Her Majesty has noticed with the liveliest feelings of gratification the manner in which the Troops of her Ally the Emperor of the French came to the aid of the Divisions of the British Army engaged in this numerically unequal contest. The Queen is deeply sensible of the cordial co-operation of the French Commander-in-Chief, General Canrobert, and the gallant conduct of that distinguished Officer, General Bosquet, and Her Majesty recognises in the cheers with which the men of both Nations encouraged each other in their united charge proofs of the esteem and admiration mutually engendered by the Campaign, and the deeds of heroism it has produced.

The Queen desires that your Lordship will

receive her thanks for your conduct throughout this noble and successful struggle, and that you will take measures for making known her no less warm approval of the services of all the Officers, Non-Commissioned Officers, and Soldiers who have so gloriously won by their blood, freely shed, fresh honours for the Army of a Country which sympathises as deeply with their privations and exertions, as it glories in their victories and exults in their fame. Let not any private soldier in those ranks believe that his conduct is unheeded—the Queen thanks him—his Country honours him.

Her Majesty will anxiously expect the further despatch in which your Lordship proposes to name those Officers whose services have been especially worthy of notice. In the meantime, I am commanded by Her Majesty to signify her approbation of the admirable behaviour of Lieutenant-General Sir George Browne, and her regret that he has been wounded in the Action. Her Majesty has received with feelings of no ordinary pleasure your Lordship's report of the matter in which Lieutenant-General His Royal Highness the Duke of Cambridge distinguished himself. That one of the Illustrious Members of Her Royal House should be associated with the toils and glories of such an Army is to the Queen a source of pride and congratulation.

To Major-General Bentinck, Major-General Codrington, Brigadier-Generals Adams, Torrens, and

Buller, your Lordship will be pleased to convey the Queen's sympathy in their wounds, and thanks for their services.

To the other Officers named by your Lordship, I am directed to express Her Majesty's approbation. The gallant conduct of Lieutenant-General Sir De Lacy Evans has attracted the Queen's especial thanks. Weak from a bed of sickness, he rose at the sound of the battle—not to claim his share in prominent command, but to aid with his veteran counsel and assistance the Junior Officer upon whom, in his absence, had devolved the duty of leading his Division.

Proud of the victory won by her brave Army—grateful to those who wear the laurels of this great conflict—the Queen is painfully affected by the heavy loss which has been incurred, and deeply sensible of what is owing to the dead. Those illustrious men cannot indeed receive the thanks of their Sovereign, which have so often cheered the Soldier in his severest trials, but their blood has not been shed in vain. Laid low in their grave of victory, their names will be cherished for ever by a grateful Country, and posterity will look upon the list of Officers who have fallen, as a proof of ardent courage and zeal with which they pointed out the path of honour to no less willing followers.

The loss of Lieutenant-General the Honourable Sir George Cathcart is to the Queen and to her People a cause of sorrow which even dims the triumph of this great occasion. His loyalty, his patriotism, and self-devotion were not less conspicuous than his high military reputation. One of a family of warriors, he was an honour to them and an ornament to his profession. Arrived in his native land from a Colony to which he had succeeded in restoring peace and contentment, he obeyed at a moment's notice the call of duty, and hastened to join that Army in which the Queen and the Country fondly hoped he would have lived to win increased renown.

The death of Brigadier-General Strangways and Brigadier-General Goldie has added to the sorrow which mingles in the rejoicing of this memorable battle.

The Queen sympathises in the loss sustained by the Families both of her Officers and Soldiers, but Her Majesty bids them reflect with her, and derive consolation from the thought, that they fell in the sacred cause of Justice and in the ranks of a Noble Army.

I have the honour to be,

My Lord,

Your Lordship's obedient humble Servant,

NEWCASTLE.

Field-Marshal
    THE LORD RAGLAN, G.C.B.,
        Etc., etc., etc.

Major-General Codrington is erroneously stated to have been wounded.

## APPENDIX.

War Department,
2nd December, 1854.

My Lord,

I have received the Queen's Commands to signify to your Lordship Her Majesty's gracious intention to confer a Medal upon all the Officers and Soldiers of the Army who have been engaged in the arduous and brilliant Campaign in the Crimea.

This Medal will bear on it the word "Crimea" with an appropriate device—a design for which has been ordered to be prepared.

It is also Her Majesty's desire that Clasps, with the names of "Alma" and "Inkerman" inscribed upon them, shall be accorded to those who have been in either, or both, of those hard fought battles, and that the same names shall in future be borne on the Colours of all the Regiments which were engaged on those bloody and glorious days.

Your Lordship will be pleased to convey to the Army this Royal Command, an additional proof of Her Majesty's appreciation of its noble services, and Her sympathy with its valour and renown.

I have the honour to be,

My Lord,

Your Lordship's obedient humble Servant,

NEWCASTLE.

Field-Marshal,
  THE LORD RAGLAN, G.C.B.,
    Etc., Etc., Etc.,
By order (Signed) J. B. B. ESTCOURT, Adj.-General.

# INDEX.

|  | PAGE |
|---|---|
| Admiral Boxer ... ... ... 123, 140, 151, 157, 188, 198, 208, | 211 |
| ,, Bruat ... ... ... ... ... ... ... ... 50, | 218 |
| ,, Dundas 18, 19, 24, 29, 47, 49, 50, 53, 61, 83, 106, 112, 114, 131, | 164 |
| ,, Freemantle ... ... ... ... ... ... ... ... | 209 |
| ,, Hamelin ... ... ... ... ... ... 49, 50, 83, 164, | 165 |
| ,, Lyons ... 18, 19, 21, 22, 23, 47, 50, 53, 61, 65, 74, 160, | 163 |
| ,, Stewart ... ... ... ... ... ... ... ... ... | 100 |
| "Agamemnon" ... ... ... ... 22, 52, 53, 65, 67, 81, 83, | 86 |
| "Albion" ... ... ... ... ... ... ... 2, 83, 84, 86, | 88 |
| Alma ... ... ... ... ... ... ... ... 56, 63, 67, 161, | 162 |
| "Andes" ... ... ... ... ... ... ... ... ... ... | 195 |
| "Arethusa" ... ... ... ... ... ... ... ... ... 86, | 88 |
| Army (Crimean Ships) ... ... ... ... ... ... ... | 136 |
| "Avon" ... ... ... ... ... ... ... ... ... ... | 109 |
| Bakery ... ... ... ... ... ... ... ... ... ... | 205 |
| Balaklava ... ... ... ... 64, 65, 69, 90, 93, 104, 142, 172, | 176 |
| ,, Battle of ... ... ... ... ... ... ... ... | 93 |
| "Banshee" ... ... ... ... ... ... ... ... ... 1, 2, | 6 |
| "Beagle" ... ... ... ... ... ... ... ... ... ... | 74 |
| "Bellerophon" ... ... ... ... ... ... ... ... 84, | 88 |
| Blockade ... ... ... ... ... ... ... ... ... ... | 44 |
| Blue book ... ... ... ... ... ... ... ... ... ... | 202 |
| Borlase ... ... ... ... ... ... ... ... ... ... | 129 |
| Bombardment (Naval) ... ... ... ... ... ... ... 84, | 164 |
| Bulgarnak ... ... ... ... ... ... ... ... ... ... | 56 |
| Burgoyne, Sir John ... ... ... ... ... ... ... ... 73, | 163 |
| Bullock hunt ... ... ... ... ... ... ... ... ... | 46 |
| Captains ... ... ... ... ... ... ... ... 106, 120, | 132 |
| ,, (merchant) ... ... ... ... ... ... ... ... 143, | 176 |
| Campaign, (General Review) ... ... ... ... ... ... | 161 |
| Campbell, Sir Colin ... ... ... ... ... ... ... ... 94, | 95 |
| "Candia" ... ... ... ... ... ... ... ... ... | 172 |
| Canrobert, General ... ... ... ... ... 4, 66, 69, 103, 131, 135, | 203 |
| Cathcart, Sir G. ... ... ... ... ... ... ... ... 102, | 124 |
| Cavalry ... ... ... ... ... ... ... ... 92, 118, 123, | 127 |
| Cardigan, Lord ... ... ... ... ... ... ... ... ... | 92 |
| Catching Russians ... ... ... ... ... ... ... ... ... | 155 |

# INDEX.

| | PAGE |
|---|---|
| Cholera ... 34, 38, 42, 45, 61, 66, 75, | 121 |
| Christie, Captain ... 145, 157, 158, 159, 175, | 187 |
| Coffee-roasting ... 121, 123, | 169 |
| Committee | 193 |
| Constantine (Fort) ... 67, 84, | 88 |
| Contrast... | 89 |
| Correspondents ... 38, 140, 175, | 184 |
| Dacres, Captain ... 52, 105, 106, 111, | 146 |
| Danube ... 10, 35, | 49 |
| "Descartes" ... 6, 7, 10, 11, | 12 |
| "Diamond" ... 67, | 193 |
| Declaration of War | 2 |
| Disembarkation ... 53, | 54 |
| Docks | 221 |
| Drummond, Captain ... 8, 11, | 136 |
| Duke of Cambridge ... 109, | 111 |
| Dunn, Lieut. ... | 84 |
| Eupatoria ... 51, | 135 |
| Expedition, Crimean ... 34, | 39 |
| ,, Odessa ... | 17 |
| ,, Sulina ... 10, | 11 |
| ,, Kertch, 1st ... | 199 |
| ,, Kertch, 2nd ... | 206 |
| ,, Kaffa ... | 23 |
| Flag of Truce ... | 3 |
| Fidonisi ... 9, | 49 |
| Filder ... 151, | 167 |
| Flank March ... 64, | 67 |
| "Firebrand" ... 15, 18, 22, 47, | 86 |
| Fishermen ... 39, 42, | 46 |
| Firewood | 175 |
| French ... 4, 49, 55, 56, 57, 59, 102, 103, 131, 135, 155, | 217 |
| "Furious" ... 3, | 8 |
| Gale ... 107, | 109 |
| Gallipoli | 4 |
| Giffard, Captain ... 25, 28, 30, | 31 |
| Goldsmith, Captain ... 11, | 39 |
| Handwriting Admiral Dundas ... | Appendix |
| Handwriting Admiral Sir E. Lyons | Do. |
| Handwriting Lord Raglan | Do. |
| Harbour Master ... 114, | 143 |
| Harbour Regulations | 176 |
| Herbert, Sidney | 166 |
| "Highflyer" ... 2, 22, 64, | 67 |
| Huts ... 138, | 151 |
| Inkerman ... 99, 124, | 165 |
| Katcha River | 162 |
| Ladies ... | 20 |

# INDEX.

245

| | PAGE |
|---|---|
| Lancaster Guns | 74, 87 |
| "Leander" | 54 |
| Louis Napoleon, Prince | 161, 200 |
| "London" | 83, 84, 85 |
| Lucan, Lord | 92 |
| McMurdo, Colonel | 185, 198 |
| Malakoff | 209, 212, 213, 220 |
| Mamalon | 212, 220 |
| Moore, Captain | 76, 78 |
| Mosquitoes | 35 |
| McNeil, Sir John | 191, 192 |
| Mules | 122, 130, 141, 151, 167 |
| Navvies | 153, 184, 186 |
| "Niger" | 3, 6, 7, 12, 18, 25, 58, 61, 66, 67, 83, 94, 106, 109 |
| Night Alarms | 95 |
| Nolan, Captain | 92, 93 |
| Odessa | 3, 6, 15, 17, 22, 26 |
| Order of Sailing and of Battle | Appendix |
| Peel, Captain | 99 |
| "Prince" | 105, 110, 141, 145, 147 |
| Powell | 27, 52, 94, 112, 117, 129, 139, 144, 175, 177 |
| Pellissier | 203, 220 |
| Pennefather | 100 |
| Principal Agent for Transports | 157 |
| Promotion | 120 |
| Prisoners | 14, 15, 28 |
| Private Signal | 38 |
| Raglan, Lord | 50, 64, 73, 92, 118, 124, 149, 153, 168, 186, 208 |
| Railroad | 134, 138, 153, 184, 185 |
| Redan | 209, 213, 216, 219, 220 |
| "Rodney" | 84 |
| Russians | 51, 57, 59, 60, 77, 155 |
| "Retribution" | 6, 10, 11, 12, 18, 85, 109 |
| Scurvy | 32 |
| "Sidon" | 10, 11 |
| St. Sophia | 33, 34 |
| Sardinians | 200, 205 |
| St. Arnaud, Marshal | 66 |
| Simpheropol | 61, 64 |
| Simpson, General | 208 |
| Sebastopol | 14, 64, 72, 183, 222 |
| "Sanspareil" | 67, 83, 86, 94, 106, 115 |
| Soyer | 205 |
| Stabling | 141, 150 |
| Stafford | 172, 174 |
| Telegraph posts | 36 |
| Tchernaya | 122 |
| "Terrible" | 15, 74 |

## INDEX.

|  |  | PAGE |
|---|---|---|
| "Tiger" | ... 25, 26, 27, 28, 29, | 31 |
| Todleben | | 219 |
| Turks | 55, 56, 92, | 122 |
| "Tribune" | 54, | 94 |
| "Queen" | 84, | 88 |
| Varna | 15, 16, 34, | 56 |
| Vesuvius | ... 24, 25, 26, 29, 38, | 94 |
| Vinois, General | | 184 |
| Visits to Camp | 72, 76, 79, 91, | 126 |
| ,, Battlefield | 59, | 100 |
| ,, French Lines | | 153 |
| ,, Sebastopol | 215, | 218 |
| Yalta | | 74 |

www.ingramcontent.com/pod-product-compliance
Lightning Source LLC
Chambersburg PA
CBHW022002160426
43197CB00007B/236